TALIA BHATT

# Trans/Rad/Fem

*Essays on Transfeminism*

Copyright © 2025 by Talia Bhatt

All rights reserved. No part of this publication may be reproduced, stored or transmitted in any form or by any means, electronic, mechanical, photocopying, recording, scanning, or otherwise without written permission from the publisher. It is illegal to copy this book, post it to a website, or distribute it by any other means without permission.

First edition

This book was professionally typeset on Reedsy.
Find out more at reedsy.com

*To my mother, who made me the woman I am today, whose flame I can only hope to live up to.*
*To my shona, whose faith in me made this book possible.*
*To my loves and my friends, without whom I could not keep fighting.*
*And to the woman reading this.*
*This one's for us all.*

# Contents

*Preface* — iii
*Praise for "Trans/Rad/Fem"* — vii

I   Part One: Fundamentals

Introduction: 'Antithesis' — 3
'Racebending' and 'Womanface': Discussing Social Constructs — 13
Understanding Transmisogyny, Part One: Misogyny and… — 20
"Heterosexuality is a Regime": On the Coercive Nature of… — 30
Understanding Transmisogyny, Part Two: Homophobia and… — 35
Understanding Transmisogyny, Part Three: Constructing the… — 44

II   Part Two: Lesbian Feminism

Understanding Lesbophobia, Part One: Diabolus ex Machina — 53
Understanding Lesbophobia, Part Two: The Machine's Final… — 66
Degendering and Regendering — 75
I Read It: The Sublime Lesbian Feminism of 'Stone Butch… — 79

III   Interlude

When the Doll Speaks — 89

IV   Part Three: Epistemicide

"Sex is Real": The Core of Gender-Conservative Anxiety    103
The Transmisogyny Bible: A Critical Dissection    107
The Third Sex    112
Conclusion: The Question Has an Answer    146

*About the Author*    166

# Preface

## Upon This Brick, I Will Break Thy Church

The first time I read Monique Wittig's *The Straight Mind,* I was sat in an autorickshaw on a busy Bandra street, making my way to the railway station.

I have had what could be described as an 'unconventional' transition journey, which began when I first learned of the term 'transgender' and of trans people at the young and tender age of "my early 20s". Despite this, I wasn't actually able to begin transitioning until I was 29. A significant chunk of my life has been spent in this state of arrested development, of being aware of what I wanted and needed to live as myself, but nonetheless denied the means and the opportunity to acquire them, year after year after year.

During this period, my only source of comfort was radical feminism.

Yes, really.

India is a sprawling beast of a nation. A region that, in its awesome totality, is referred to as a 'subcontinent' for good reason. The sheer diversity in language, culture, cuisine, and experience from region to region, let alone state to state, is dizzying, overwhelming, resistant to the very notion of encapsulation. Even having spent more than two decades of my life there, even having grown up there, I cannot reasonably claim to fully fathom its every corner, its every nuance.

Yet, I feel absolute certainty when declaring that wherever you go in India, it will be intensely patriarchal.

The biggest disconnect between myself and the Western readers my work aims to reach is almost certainly this gulf, where I have seen misogyny thrive in nearly every context imaginable. Whether amidst professional academics on the East Coast or autorickshaw drivers in Udaipur, I've observed just how casual, thoughtless, everyday, and embedded into the very substrate of social life misogyny is. I'm not even referring to sentiments directed at me, necessarily, just a comment here, an assumption there, angry rants about how unreasonable wives are sprinkled throughout.

Perhaps the most amusing interactions I've had involve the (mis)use of that oft-vaunted yet scarcely-read theory, 'intersectionality'. More than once, I've opened social media to be chided by a woman who's never so much as visited my country on how "white feminist" my ideas are. That I should, yet again, read *that* paper on 'intersectionality'. The one that I've already read and my interlocutors usually haven't, so that I might fully grasp how reductive it is to assert that men exploit women under patriarchy. After all, would I really claim that *white women* oppress *men of color*?

"What a fascinating question," I tend to remark. "I have one of my own, if you would care to ponder it for a moment?"

"In societies that aren't locally white-hegemonic and multiracial—in patriarchal cultures all over the third world, for example, do 'men of color' oppress 'women of color'?"

To date, I haven't received a calm answer to my question, leave alone an actual apology.

Crenshaw's *Demarginalizing the Intersection of Race and Sex* rather explicitly highlights the frequent erasure of women of color from conversations regarding both racism and feminism, for the record. It discusses at length the manner in which we are asked to "choose", to "declare our allegiance", as though we could in any reasonable sense subdivide aspects of us that constitute the sum total of our oppression in a white-supremacist, patriarchal context.

Most published feminist theory is from a white, Western perspective because the women most likely to be academically and economically positioned to produce it have been white and/or Western. (And cis and straight, for that matter.) A lot of even pop-feminist output, the everyday discourses that occur between women in non-rigorous contexts, suffers from the further myopia of taking the West's recent feminist gains for granted. It was certainly amusing to read papers on "postfeminism" produced by scholars who seem unaware of how prevalent arranged and forced marriages remain the world over, including within their own backyards, though I admit that the novelty has long worn off.

Radical feminism was the first school of feminist thought I encountered that seemed unafraid to look the visceral reality of existing as a woman in the eye, without flinching. It helped me give voice to those deeply-rooted feelings of rage, despair, and the unabating sense of injustice that characterizes being aware of patriarchal atrocities. The modern discursive landscape regards the feminist as a retired dinosaur, a gauche, imposing, unwelcome, and rather rude figure unwilling to cease with her hysterics. Don't you know that to insist on the centrality of misogyny to society's very organization, to the essential fabric of reactionary thought, is neither sufficiently *intersectional* nor *decolonial?*

Don't you know that claiming "women are an oppressed class" is *gender essentialism?*

That is, ultimately, the argument I encountered the most, and the one that most stirringly moved me to break my silence. Tweet by tweet. Essay by essay. And, now, book by book. A clear, materialist analysis of how misogyny animates patriarchal society or a robust model of the social construction of sex is not *bioessentialism*. Rather, it is the best framework we have for understanding the basis of cissexism and transphobia.

These non-critiques are widespread because while "trans rights" is a fashionable thing to declare your support for these days—though of course, news media is working overtime to change that—actually doing the work to empathize with trans people, trans women particularly, is ... effort. Especially if you haven't quite grasped what "sex is a social construct" is even supposed to mean, or still think that trans women have lived typically male lives right up until the point we decided to put on a dress.

Ultimately, that is the blunt, paradigm-shattering thesis of this book. The trans woman has for too long been held up as a symbol for cis society to alternatively pity, cum to, and burn in effigy. We are a hot topic to have an opinion on but not a sufficiently humanized population whose plight matters on its own merits. We are a curiosity, a paradox, a fun thought experiment in a gender studies class, but are we really worth taking seriously?

Are we *really* women?

Within this tome, I present to you a year's worth of contentious, arduous, and sometimes backbreaking work. A project oriented around plugging linguistic gaps, formulating frameworks, and giving both transfeminists and those who seek a better understanding of trans issues the tools to properly elucidate how transmisogyny functions. It is not the be-all and end-all of declaring the trans woman a firmly feminist subject, in a manner that should have been obvious to the 'greatest' thinkers on gender and queerness.

No, it is very much only the beginning. That, I promise.

I hold no reverence for your idols. I declare no allegiance to your priests. I do not honor the sanctity of your temples. I am not a shield for excusing the violence of men, nor a convenient scapegoat to butcher in their stead. I am neither an excuse to prop up antifeminist sentiment nor am I a voiceless puppet for whom others must speak.

I'm a fucking tranny with something to say, here to remind you that we used to be regarded as oracles for a reason.

# Praise for "Trans/Rad/Fem"

"Talia Bhatt's writing is a revelation, a revindication, and a razor-sharp dissection of the ways that patriarchy, Western chauvinism, and transmisogyny have deeply influenced most contemporary approaches to feminism and queer and trans liberation. In crackling prose that encompasses both intellectual clarity and deep feeling, Bhatt draws from both lived experience and academic expertise to clearly illuminate a vision of radical feminism that perceives trans women, trans lesbians, and those forced into "third sex" categories as full human beings rather than political symbols or objects of projection. Bhatt fearlessly and gracefully takes apart many assumptions that have become core to liberal and neoliberal approaches to queer and trans activism, such as the notion of a "gender binary" that must be overturned and the Orientalist fantasy of gender utopian pre-colonial societies - and in doing so, opens up the possibility of liberation work that is rooted in deeper solidarity and greater revolutionary potential. I wish that I could send this book back in time to my younger self - and to all the trans women longing for a clearer reflection of our lives. This is a book that is sure to reshape the discourse on trans femininity, and it stands powerfully alongside the work of thinkers such as Vivian Namaste, Mirha Soleil-Ross, and Julia Serano."

- Kai Cheng Thom, author of *Fierce Femmes and Notorious Liars*

I

## Part One: Fundamentals

*Establishing a basis for our discussions of transmisogyny, through the lens of a materialist transfeminism. This part begins with a personal essay, 'Antithesis', which I had hoped would be the only personal essay in the collection. My future work made me re-evaluate that desire.*

# Introduction: 'Antithesis'

*"If god existed, it would be necessary to destroy him."*

I have a rather fraught relationship with my mother.

Already I can hear the shifts in disposition, the collective groans from some and gleeful grins from others as I merrily type the single worst opening sentence a trans woman can possibly confess in an essay about her transition, her journey, her identity. Sexologists, in particular, love mothers, love the availability of so ready a scapegoat, a proximate woman to blame for a (presumed) man's sickening, emasculating deviancies. Whether in explaining male homosexuality or transsexuality, our phantom mothers have always stood at our backs, their masculine deficiencies and feminine excesses staining us in equal measure, making us more woman-like than any respectable, untainted man should rightly be.

You can almost see sweat pouring off knitted brows, the frenzied clawing of nib against paper as sexologists compulsively tear away at sentence after sentence of condemnation, spittle flying with every written-and-recited-word to pathologize our mothers—never fathers—desperate to declare us all perverse, aberrant abnormalities so very unlike them, so very *different* and apart, because they could never ever be like us and being like us was *wrong* it *had* to be there was no way that we could ever inhabit the sanctified realm of the *natural*.

I digress.

Most stories start at the beginning and you'd think mine would too, to which I'd have to ask: which beginning? The first time someone referred to me as a woman in loving instead of mocking terms, and it felt like stumbling indoors after an interminable stint wandering around in thick, choking fog? Or the first time I was forced to leave class in the middle of the day and have my supposedly too-long hair haphazardly slashed at by a barber with rough and calloused fingers, pushing down the horror that mounted with every receding inch, feeling like my armor, my cloak, my best feature was being shorn off for no reason I could name other than petty authoritarian cruelty?

My English wife thinks that I had more of an English private school education than she did despite growing up in Mumbai, what with the gender-segregated uniforms and stringent rules about short hair and shining shoes and the inane conformity that served no purpose other than to cut off all avenues for self-expression from growing children, and manufacturing banal excuses to punish them. I rather agree.

It's hard to question things in such an environment, not because the questions aren't there, but because asking them is punished, doing anything other than exactly what you're told is punished. You want to ask and the question dies in your throat. You want to imagine other ways of being, but you have to wake up groggy at the crack of dawn and put on your boy shoes and boy belt and boy shirt and, most importantly, your big boy pants. Stand in the boy line, sit with the boy groups, do the boy activities, get harassed by the boys in the boy bathroom when you're trying to change because you're too "shy" and "reserved" and "quiet" and other adjectives that are not exactly "effeminate and insufficiently boy-like" but amount to them anyway, to the point where you begin to viscerally, physically dread the days when you have to change into the bloody Physical Ed shorts and you start wearing them under your trousers so at least no one will try to pry off your fucking underwear while they have the chance.

No questions were brooked, but there's a lot of answers there, now that I look.

Pity's not what I seek. A narrative, yes, that's something I'm building deliberately. If you want something to be digested, it needs a beginning, a middle and an end, doubly so if it's something complex and you really need the most important bits to be distilled, to get across and be absorbed despite the many dozen confounding and contributing factors you have to leave out for brevity's sake. Think about what's most crucial, and think about the simplest terms to explain it without losing any nuance. I think about that sort of thing a lot. You become obsessed with structure and meaning and packing in the most information you can when everything you say growing up carries with it a risk of punishment, whether that's a slap across the face or curses screamed at you or nails digging into your skin with fury. Or later down the line, a racist dismissal of perfectly clear speech, being marked down for "mispronouncing" a word that was merely accented.

I speak with an American accent now. My wife hates it. Calls me a yank when I'm being snotty.

A part of me considers this something of a pointless exercise. There is less value to pouring your heart out, to narrating a personal journey than there is in explaining things, in at least trying to describe complex interlocking social phenomena that feed back into each other in straightforward if byzantine ways. Yet oftentimes, when I hear the popular narratives that have popped up around trans womanhood, I can't help but feel like I'm listening to someone describe a similar trip to a favorite vacation spot rather than something I instantly recognize and see my own experience reflected within. I did not take that route, I usually go by train. The berths are largely empty, it usually runs deserted. So let's find a point, if we can. Let me tell you how a trans woman realizes herself without feeling like she was born in the wrong body, without longing for the sweet boys who never gave her a second look in the hallways.

India's culture is extremely gendered.

It is best explained in harsh economic and legal terms: the labor force participation gap between men and women is catastrophic. Hindu women, comprising the majority in a nation whose property laws vary by religion, did not have equal inheritance rights to men until 2005, and even after are frequently coerced to give up their claims by male family members. To restrict income, financial rights and property is to not merely confine women to the domestic sphere, it is to shackle them perennially to fathers and brothers and husbands, to bind up their destinies with the closest available man. Domestic abuse has laughably little recourse, legally or otherwise, especially in a culture that considers these private matters and harshly punishes women for reporting it at all. Marital rape is legal.

Rape, as a whole, sometimes feels legal.

Not that legality really counts for that much in a post-colonial ruin suffering from nationwide abjection. Laws seem to matter most around urban centers, where those who cannot pay bribes find themselves restricted by them, while rapidly decreasing in relevancy the further from cities you retreat. Some places still burn widows on their husbands' pyres, while others abandon them to poverty. Child marriage remains rampant. So does the supposedly illegal practice of dowry. Communities supersede things as trite and banal as federal laws in India, and communities bow to patriarchs, to their traditions, to their ancestral ways of doing things. As such, the various burdens of siring a girl instead of a prized *son* cause infanticide to remain pervasive. Those who lack the stomach to outright drown their infant girls in milk still neglect, starve and abuse them. Many never make it to adulthood.

I do not understand how, as I sit here and type this, there are no flames pouring out of my mouth.

All this to say that while gender may be *present* no matter where you go, it is *palpable* in India. It forms the fabric of everyday existence in a way that is inescapable, undeniable, and if considered in its totality, utterly and overwhelmingly maddening. I wonder, sometimes, if the eldritch tomes of forbidden knowledge that crop up in so many Lovecraftian jaunts, driving any reader to gibbering, irreconcilable lunacy within minutes of perusal, were simply feminist texts with accompanying statistics.

There are expectations in such an environment, ways of carrying yourself and behaving that you must exhibit, lest you become subject to ridicule, to ostracisation, to being marked permanently as the boy everyone else gets to torment. 'Sensitive' was a word thrown around by teachers and adults who expressed concern but still seemed to lack interest in actually intervening. Some even joined in, for reasons that escaped me at the time but seem the slightest bit clearer today. The nuances of bravado, machismo, of imbibing the superiority that was allegedly my birthright always escaped me, even as an act, even insincerely. There did not appear to be a way to reconcile what I was with what I was supposed to be, no way to cross the ever-widening chasm between myself and my supposed peers.

My mother likely felt no less alone.

It was a strange experience, moving back home to care for my ailing father. Cleaning his bedpan, cooking him meals he rejected for the flimsiest reasons, watching him slowly waste away, all the while having no recourse to the things he subjected my mother to. You feel trapped, like you have to stay to intercede regardless of how little difference it makes, even as all the decades of frustration and bitterness and tears and anger are redirected away from him and onto you, like they always have been. I lived in a house where the one who raised her hand the most wasn't the one who did the most damage, because the central conceit of manhood is a complete lie. It's not about strength. It doesn't matter how big you are, how bulky and stocky and well-built. What matters, what has always mattered, is who holds the power, who has the ability to turn who out onto the streets and thereby keep them in line.

Mom was always a very angry woman.

Would you believe me if I told you this was her best quality? I told her once through gritted teeth that all she ever gave me was this useless pit of anger, but I lied. It isn't useless. Anger is the fire that keeps you warm in the bitter cold of meandering, hazy roads, the bright, burning beacon that lights your way no matter how murky. Rage at your conditions, your treatment, your circumstances can keep you upright, keep you sane, keep you alive, keep you putting one foot in front of another when little else will. So many women suffer because they were never permitted to feel their rage, because they had it smothered and choked out young, because they weren't allowed to be angry at what was being done to them. My mother, bless her, wasn't like that. She kept her fire lit.

Until she couldn't.

Thirty odd years is a long time, after all.

You have to tell yourself these things, I suppose. You have to tell yourself you were happy, then, you were always happy through the hard times and the harder times. You have to convince yourself that the man who slaved your existence to his own didn't hollow you out, didn't reduce you to a shell of the woman you might have been without him. Have to, because imagining that woman is in and of itself painful, not to mention nearly impossible in a culture so unforgiving and cruel to unbound women. What else could she have been, I think she reasons. At least she had her life.

At least she had her son.

Me, I've never been able to lie to myself quite like that. To others, certainly, insofar as keeping a stony countenance whenever you're called something you're not is dishonesty. My father's bier needed his son's shoulder, so that he may be laid to rest in peace. I did him that last kindness. Then, as the flames rose up to consume him, I placed my male self atop his corpse and left my old life behind in his ashes.

Don't you like that imagery? I quite do. Gives the mess of my life a certain dramatic *heft*. Phoenixes and flames and purification, and all that. Maybe I'm better at lying to myself than I thought I was.

Insofar as you can declare such a thing at 30-odd years old, my story has a happy ending. I live with the love of my life, I have finally transitioned and I now get to be the woman that my culture, and patriarchal-culture-at-large, tried to extinguish. I'm a lesbian happily married to a lesbian who helps me, heals me and completes me in a way no one ever has, nourishing me with a love I had at one point given up all hope of ever experiencing. To go from spending most of my twenties in near total social and geographic isolation from others like me, to living the life I never thought I would be able to is nothing short of a miracle, one that she made possible.

Which is where you might think this ought to conclude. After all, I gave you a beginning. You're at the end. Should not the journey be complete?

Maybe it should. Though some of you might have realized by now, or had the discomfiting feeling while I rather stereotypically gushed about my wife: I forgot to give you a middle.

Didn't I?

Truthfully, if my little narrative reads as oddly contiguous, that's because it is. I could easily assemble a more consonant tale from my personal history if I tried, centering the unexpected "eureka!" moment of my life where I went from learning about transness in adulthood (India is quite conservative, as you may recall, and was only more so several decades ago) to realizing that *I*, myself, could be trans ... several *years* later. Given that even after that realization, I still had to spend several *more* years with no ability to act on my revelation, not until I had a modicum of independence and control over my own destiny, that moment itself seems oddly quaint and immaterial in hindsight. A fleeting spark that could have come from any of a dozen sources, itself insignificant in the overarching picture.

No, there's nothing quite so clean about the impetus to transition, no past spent playing with dolls or trying on dresses that I can foreground as easy justification. I would be lying if I attempted to claim an unfulfilled affinity for femininity, or a deeply-held desire to see a different face in the mirror. I've always quite liked my face, in all honesty, if not the thick hairs that used to encroach upon it. I've always thought it was pretty. I have often been told that I'm the spitting image of my mother.

What actually compelled me to transition, then, was the same feeling I've harbored all my life, the same corrosive wrongness that I experienced as years upon years of swallowing poison, of being force-fed an unacceptable ideology until I had no choice but to puke it all up. I, simply put, could not be a man. I refused.

I REFUSE to be a man.

I **REFUSE** to be a man.

This is an uncomfortable thing for people to hear, in my experience, and I've only ever rarely found others who would describe their desire to transition in this way. When trying to see if any others shared this sentiment, I'm usually instead told that identity should be *affirmative*. "I was always a woman" is something that's never resonated though, because while I've been surrounded by womanhood, grown up loving women familially and romantically and all sorts of ways I don't even have names for, I also was keenly aware that 'woman' was something I wasn't. There had always been a thick barrier between myself and womanhood, and no matter how beaten-bloody my fists were against it, it remained unimpeachable.

While the thing I was supposed to be, the thing I was being forced to be, was something I simply could not abide.

Manhood is not a natural state of being, no matter how many preachers and pick-up artists ardently insist that sexual domination is stored in the balls. It is not natural, not inevitable, and certainly not biological destiny for a boy to burn away all the parts that feel empathy, to harbor and nourish a disdain for girls until they've become objects to consume and possess and communally debate the worth of with fellow men. Devaluation, denigration, these are behaviors that are *taught*, an ideology that our cultures are all immersed in and one that we are coercively expected to reproduce. Misogyny and male supremacy form the basis of our oldest institutions and seep into all the facets of everyday existence, from whose opinions hold the most weight to how we love and how we care and how we fuck. It is omnipresent, like being plunged into a putrescent, overflowing septic tank.

But you can still swim to the surface.

I do understand why, in a society still steeped in patriarchy, speaking about the rejection of manhood and the decentering of it from one's life so regularly invites anger and backlash. Even now, when I call myself a lesbian and stress my lack of attraction to men, I am met with a truly bewildering amount of hostility for expressing something borderline definitional. I have been accused of everything from biphobia to gatekeeping, with some going so far as to darkly insinuate that my own transness makes my rejection of (there is an unspoken "other") men myopic in some way. You could almost feel a sense of anticipation among people, waiting for me to be hoisted by my own petard, for my own man-exclusion to come back and bite me because apparently, my birth sex inducted me into a lifelong allegiance to the category 'man' whether I want it or not.

Fuck that. I'm not a coward.

Repudiating the societal imperative to embrace manhood may not be comfortable, may not be easy and may invite harsh repercussions, but it's the only principle that can form the core of an effective feminism. It does no one any good to bleat about how 'everyone' suffers under a system of oppression, eliding that not everyone suffers *equally*. Some of us are more invested in patriarchy than others, materially benefit from its maintenance and have a greater stake in upholding it, in resisting any attempts to undermine its edicts and continued existence. You cannot actively resist any form of bigotry without being clear-eyed about this reality, without being willing to admit that there are *oppressors* who benefit from participating in oppression. Promises of a future of greater benefits after liberation ring hollow in the ears of those who benefit from oppression *now*.

That's the truth I've always held at the burning-hot core of my identity. To love women, to really love them and be with them, you can't not hate that which hurts them. A love that doesn't inspire ceaseless rage at injustice, inequity, harm and dismissal isn't much of a love at the end of the day.

Societal hierarchies are founded on violence and abuse, on those afforded subjectivity and prominence and those denied it. Subjugation to the whims, desires and demands of men is so universal an aspect of womanhood that even women's media and marketing oriented towards them highlight this as a given, an unshakeable constant in what being Woman means. Rom coms and "chick flicks" are about finding and being with men. Make-up and fashion and beauty about being desirable to men. Even transformative fiction, a realm of putatively limitless creation, inevitably centers around sexuality that purports to be subversive but inevitably orbits the central topic of men. A colonization of the imagination in addition to the material.

Does patriarchy hurt men? Maybe. But it hurts women *first*.

That's the part that matters.

It can be tempting, when discussing matters as lofty as liberation, to indulge in a little utopianism, to want to imagine what a glorious post-gender world may look like. Perhaps it's heartening to think of a world where anatomy carries with it no social connotation, no implicit sorting of human beings into "master" and "lesser" based on assumed biological destiny alone. Knowing and reminding yourself of the new world you're fighting for can be a source of strength when the old world, in its death throes, assiduously strives to destroy it in utero.

Even so, one must ensure the old world actually *dies*. Every unjust hierarchy must end, and this one, this oldest and closest and most ubiquitous one, must end most of all. The entrails of the last Priest must serve as a noose for the last King whose sword must be buried in the bosom of the last Patriarch. Until then, women will not be free. Manhood as an ideology must be abolished.

My story and my own approach to my identity won't be particularly popular or palatable, I think. So much of it is contentious, rooted in the kind of rationale that alarmists and conformists would only be too happy to exploit. There is no shortage of people willing to hold societal violence over queer women's heads, to pathologize our identities as trauma-induced, to insist that we are transsexual or gay or anything else they can't grapple with because men hurt us or our fathers hurt us or we had, heaven forfend, too much empathy for our mothers. To which I can only say one thing.

So what?

So what if that's what happened?

'Normal' society is irredeemable. Barbaric.

There's nothing wrong with being like me if the alternative is being like *them*.

# 'Racebending' and 'Womanface': Discussing Social Constructs

"Why can't you transition from one race to another?"

That's not a trick question, I promise. If you've ever encountered it in the wild, usually on social media, it will most likely have been phrased as one, no doubt, and more than likely in a context that is meant to delegitimize the existence of transgender people, or call the validity of our identities into question. Transphobes tend to invoke a kind of *reductio ad absurdum* that makes sense only if you've already bought into their premises, and much of their 'argumentation' relies on stating truths about (trans)gendered existence in a mocking tone under the assumption that, when faced with how utterly farcical the conclusions of trans-acceptance are, people will completely abandon it as the ludicrous idea it so *obviously* is.

Still, I'd invite you to think about this question, because it's a sticky one. Most people understand on a certain level that transitioning between genders makes more inherent sense than "transitioning" between races, that the latter is indeed quite preposterous, but they probably couldn't tell you *why*. Which is where the gleeful transphobic line of attack jumps right back in: *"Oh, they're both social constructs, are they not? If gender and race are both made-up, if you can discard your assigned gender, why not do the same with your 'assigned' race?"*

Let's sit with that for a moment. I honestly encourage you to think about this argument before continuing to read, because the core equivalency it relies on is an important one to explore and deconstruct.

One thing about this claim ought to stand out: the idea that because 'race' and 'gender' are both 'social constructs', they are equivalent in some fundamental way and therefore must share essential properties and be reasoned about similarly. Crucially, what this argument really wants to assert is that if a progressive social model truly wishes to regard both race and gender as independent of and unmoored by biology, then what applies for one should also apply for the other. It's *reductio ad absurdum* again, one that relies upon an instinctual rejection of the idea that one can change their race. If you, as a progressive, think that the idea of a white person transitioning to Black or Asian or any other race is absurd, you must then also realize that the idea of transition between genders is *equally* absurd. If you don't, then you have a contradiction in your worldview, and you are required to explain why you feel so differently about the supposed 'arbitrariness' of race versus that of gender.

A part of me actually quite likes this argument, because it's almost based in sound logical principles. Rather than simple name-calling or decreeing some progressive ideal as against 'common sense', it's an actual attempt to engage with the worldview and try to expose a flaw in it. Rhetorically it is a question that almost demands an answer, some justification for why these two cases are dissimilar.

Too bad the core reasoning is based on a complete misunderstanding of what a 'social construct' is.

Race and gender are indeed both social constructs, but so are the number of hours that divide a day, the number of days that comprise a 'week', the notion of 'currency' and 'nations', and the very language that you're currently reading this essay in. All of those concepts being socially constructed does not make them equivalent, else a promise today would be as good a payment for a hamburger as cash on Tuesday. The actual sticky wicket is that most people don't understand what a social construct is particularly well, past perhaps grasping the idea that it connotes something *intangible* and therefore *immaterial*.

Every social construct is thus violently collapsed into a singular, false equivalency—that is, they are considered to be "made up"—and asserting that something is a social construct can conveniently be discarded, ignored, or declared a ridiculous argument in some way, because the thing under discussion is obviously *real*. To a gender-conservative, whose core project has always involved the naturalization of the binary gendered hierarchy, you might as well call gender a "figment of the imagination", despite the fact that feminist theory knows all too well just how concrete and material gendered social relations truly are. We might then do well to not fall into this same misconception, and understand what a social construct actually *is*.

Simply put, a social construct is an abstraction that derives meaning by consensus.

Well, maybe that's more 'concise' than 'simple'. Starting from the more basic examples and working our way up, we see that a lot of social constructs are 'agreements', a way to establish a common understanding of a socially-relevant idea. Think of measurements: how long a meter is, how much time elapses in one minute, what sub-divisions and units we need in order to standardize and disseminate information in a systematic, regular manner—these are all things that require *consensus*, a common understanding of 'seconds' and 'liters' and exactly how many notches there should be in a ruler. These are all "made up", yes, in the most technical sense, but that makes them neither meaningless nor totally divorced from the material. A 'meter' has the meaning it does because we've given it that meaning, and it does indeed describe something tangible: distance.

This applies equally to less concretized notions, like a 'community' or a 'nation'. 'Nationhood' only takes the measure of someone in extremely binary terms—whether one is a member of that nation or not—but brings with it a whole host of presumptions and connotations, of being 'from' a particular geographic bound, of growing up with a particular shared culture and history, of speaking certain languages and not others and oftentimes of bearing certain, specific animosities. Socially-constructed though it is, 'nationhood' carries with it many material inferences. The line on a map that cleaves one state from another may have no real-world equivalent in the actual landscape, but the bullets one would accrue in one's back for attempting to cross it without proper authorization are fatally real all the same.

Keeping this in mind, we may already have our answer. Why do the rules for 'gender' not apply to 'race' as well? Because gender and race are not the same concept. They are different ideas, different constructions and they connote vastly different things. One could walk into a room and announce that they were race-transitioning and it would be just as meaningful a statement as claiming that their race is 'about seventy degrees Fahrenheit' or 'the Gregorian Calendar'.

Though, I surmise that while that's certainly *true*, it's not a satisfying answer, is it? We know race and gender are different, but could we expand upon how? What makes one more ephemeral than the other?

If race is an abstraction, what exactly is it abstracting?

There is an axiom that has been so far implicit to this exercise that is best made explicit: that we will primarily be discussing 'race' from a Western, largely US-centric perspective. That is the context within which 'race' is most meaningful, and theirs is the conception of race that is most commonly exported and understood, even in nations where other social divisions are more important and relevant. This juxtaposition of 'race' and '(trans)gender' is a largely Western phenomenon regardless, so it really won't alter the context of the conversation to state this plainly.

Consider, now, what 'social function' race fulfills in the West, what the social consequences of race are in Western culture and society. One purpose is *homogenizing*—European settlers in what is now the US, all from various nations and regions, adopted 'whiteness' as a unifying social category, one that distinguished them both from the indigenous populations whose lands they were colonizing and the Africans upon whose commodified labor and bodies their settler-colony was eventually built. Similarly in the modern context, race blurs significant lines in order to cohere various groups into homogenous categories, usually reflecting the Western contextual understanding of or interest in those groups. In South Asia, for example, though religion and nationality are the significant social divides and carry a great degree of importance, an Indian, a Pakistani and a Bangladeshi would still all be considered 'brown' to the Western eye, despite the likelihood that those people would consider their identities and experiences as quite distinct from one another.

These broad categories are also reflective of a certain legal and social standing within Western culture. Whiteness is generally privileged while members of other races face worse socio-economic outcomes, reflecting a certain status within the West's racial hierarchy. Historically this has been reflected in actual law and remains de facto true even now, despite many such laws being dismantled.

Race therefore codifies a certain relationship with Western *citizenhood*, whether one is considered a *first*-class citizen or not. It is a proxy, in some sense, of who may be a 'true' citizen of the implicitly-white 'nation'. A non-white person may be an immigrant with legal, naturalized status, or someone whose family has been in the West for generations, but they can still be considered less of a citizen—regardless of their legal or social standing—due to their position in the racial hierarchy.

This social positionality is not merely extant, however, but *historical*, or *ancestral*. Racial status was itself something determined by an assumed relationship to specific historical events and forces, forming an association between a non-white person and certain histories of colonization, slavery, or genocide. Race then, implicitly becomes a way to encode these historical violences, in a way being mobilized to demarcate the imperialized from the citizens of empire, the colonizers from the colonized.

If this seems reductive, that's partly because race *is* a reductive category. An East Asian person could be descended from a family that has lived in the United States since the 19th century, while a white person might be a naturalized immigrant from Canada or France. This possibility still does not stop the term 'immigrant' from being racialized in specific ways or from being deployed as a cudgel against certain populations. Racial status, in many regards, reduces the non-white individual to their position in the Western racial hierarchy, thereby treating them as the perpetual Other, the perpetual outsider unable to access true legitimacy under the national project. ("Citizenship" as a legitimizing social construct itself is predicated upon certain violences mobilized against those without access to such legitimacy, in ways that are invariably racialized too!)

Hilariously, if we were willing to stretch a metaphor, there **is** a 'racial' analogue to gender transition that we could make, one that bears surprising similarities to the social response to gender transition: changing citizenship. Think about it: You could 'transition' from 'Indian' or 'Kenyan' or 'Indonesian' to 'US-American' legally but still not be considered a legitimate Westerner due to essentialized biological characteristics, which perennially mark you as a member of your 'birth race/nation' and can be used to demean your equal standing!

This is a metaphor that is admittedly stretched to breaking point but does show some interesting analogues between race and gender without collapsing the two, of which the primary common feature is a conservative desire to *essentialize social categories in the realm of the biological.* 'Whiteness' cannot simply connote a higher status under imperial logics, it must necessarily constitute *racial superiority*, must regard differences in socioeconomic outcomes as a *natural consequence* of greater capability in some races against others. Skin colors and certain features *must* be correlated to intelligence, competence, ability, proficiency, and must necessarily supersede centuries of historical ravaging and plunder and exploitation!

Which brings us to the final nail in the coffin for racial-gendered juxtaposition: History itself. An individual could perhaps alter their biological characteristics enough—or already be born with paler skin and more Eurocentric features than other members of their race—but they could never transition out of their lineage, or their historical positionality within the periphery or the West's internal colonies, any more than they could alter the timeline itself. Race, in the final calculus, is a much more temporally-deterministic social category, one that ultimately doesn't simply describe how you currently look and how you are currently treated within society, but that necessarily echoes through previous generations and their (mis)treatment, their exploitation, their impoverishment. You cannot transition to the Gregorian Calendar, to an economic class you don't have the wealth for, or out of an existing history of subjugation. To do so would require uprooting the various class-supremacist ideologies that underpin our entire modern existence.

In contrast to this, gender is *much* more grounded in one's present existence. The gendered binary constructed and upheld by patriarchy divides all people into two categories, marking one for domestic, sexual, and reproductive exploitation by the other based on their respective presumed biodestinies. Binary gender encodes heterosexuality as a regime and is meant to enforce who one is permitted to partner with as well as the expected role one is meant to perform within that partnership, a social reality that is much easier to contravene, to betray, to walk away from in the here and now.

I hope this exploration of social constructs and the differing social meanings of race and gender was edifying in some way and was at least easy to follow and understand. Transphobes in general really want to be able to 'unveil' gender transition as a ridiculous, impossible farce, a reactionary desire that is itself a result of a poor understanding of how gender is socially constructed and a denial of how trans people can and do materially alter their sex and gender positionality. Don't be tricked into believing that *we're* the ones ignoring the blatant truth in front of our eyes.

# Understanding Transmisogyny, Part One: Misogyny and Heterosexualism

This is perhaps a controversial sentiment, but most people have a very surface-level understanding of misogyny.

This is ultimately a fate shared by most bigotries, as conceptualized by the average person: "I don't *hate* the gays. I don't *hate* non-whites. I don't *hate* women!" Which might even be true, since most people tend to not be ideologically committed to the active hatred of certain demographics. All the same, they might still pull their child out of the local public school when they notice that the student body has become disproportionately full of children from "poorer neighborhoods" (as a safety measure! Private school might be a better fit anyway). Or they might happily attend a drag brunch but become incredibly uncomfortable if they find out that their child has a gay friend, or isn't quite as interested in the opposite sex as they should be, at that age. They might even be ardently pro-choice and advocate for equal pay, but remain vigilant and suspicious of any woman their husband befriends or seems to get too close to—most women are envious and covetous, after all, and it would be naive foolishness to not safeguard the happiness you worked so hard to build.

(Did you think the misogynist I was describing in gender-neutral terms was a man this whole time? Perhaps you should check your implicit biases—women can be misogynists too!)

In general, systemic bigotry is far more deeply-rooted than mere personal acrimony. Woman-hatred at the interpersonal level is nowhere near the totality of *misogyny*, a system that is most likely our oldest institution, one embedded into the cultural, the political, and the economic as much as the personal or the private spheres. Misogyny is a *regime*, an organizing principle of society itself, one that dictates and pervades nearly all aspects of social life. We can ask, then, what is the matrix that births this force, this machine? What is the *function* of misogyny?

Succinctly, misogyny is the organizing principle by which heterosexuality is reproduced.

Admittedly, that's a bit of a mouthful, and confusing in its own regard if one's understanding of heterosexuality is 'attraction to the opposite sex'. That short statement is in and of itself quite illustrative, however: think of 'opposite sexes' as a phrase, how it implies not merely the binary of sex, but also how it juxtaposes them, frames them as *opposites, antagonistic, polarized*. That alone should begin to reveal something about the deeper structures at play, how the role of 'man' and 'woman' are constructed in our lexicon and imbued with meaning far beyond the merely biological.

For the biological is where the traditional, conservative and simplistic notion of gender begins and ends. To the gender-conservative, a man is a man due to the penis and testicles he is born with, while a woman is a woman due to her vagina, her womb, her breasts, all the aspects of her biological make-up that make her innately oriented towards motherhood and the rearing of the young. Gender is thus self-evident, even banal and mundane, a straightforward matter of biological destiny determined at birth. Some of us are birthers and some of us are sires, which is where the matter ends.

Only, that's not where it ends at all. It would be one thing if gender was merely an imprecise determinant of one's reproductive capability, but everyone who lives under patriarchy is intimately familiar with how much *more* it connotes, how much about your life and ambitions and permitted disposition is dictated by gender. Gender carries with it a *social* meaning as well, a socially-imposed bevy of characteristics and expectations that individuals of that gender are asked to meet.

A woman is not merely a person with the reproductive potential to give birth, to gestate and deliver a child. She is also a *nurturer*, someone *soft* and *caring* and *loving* and *understanding*, who is suited for the demands of the *domestic*, the *household*, the **selfless** imperative to feed and clothe and teach and raise others without regard to her own wants and desires. A woman is a *homemaker*, is *weaker* and *less assertive* and *naturally inclined to follow*, someone who *craves submission*, who *requires leadership*, who needs to be *led* and will allow herself to be, once someone who demonstrates that he (invariably a 'he') can lead her takes 'command' of her. All of these traits, these *roles* assigned to women in the social realm of the patriarchal society, do not flow naturally from the mere fact of perhaps being born with gestational anatomy, but gender-traditionalists are extremely invested in the notion that they do.

As for men, they are conversely *independent*, natural-born *leaders* and *dominants* for whom the imposition of their will upon nature and other people is an innate urge, an unquenchable biological *drive*. Men are strong! Sturdy! Rigid! Turgid! Inseparable from the romanticization of the phallic and its inevitable poetic derivatives, meant to embody qualities such as *stalwart* and *stoic* and *dependable* and *powerful*. It seems that the desire for freedom and autonomy, along with all the attendant intellectual and physiological auspices that are indelibly associated with that desire, is stored in the balls.

Ludicrous as that proposition is, it remains the ideological fixation and overarching societal project of gender conservatism. You can easily see, then, why assertive women or men attracted to other men or any and all exceptions to the socially-prescribed gender orthodoxy invites such deep-seated antipathy and hostility. It is an inflexible categorization that must be maintained at all costs, that must be rooted in our 'natural', 'evolutionary wiring', lest any opposition to these limiting, arbitrary social categories gain any legitimacy!

Already, the answer to our question regarding the basic purpose of misogyny is taking shape. We have a great many of the pieces—the biological differentiation of the sexes that is imbued with undue social meaning, the confinement of women to one sphere contrasted with the autonomy and self-determination afforded men—but we still need to put the full picture together. The missing piece here, the one connecting the construction of strictly-differentiated social gender roles with the underlying motivation, is *heterosexuality*.

In the social realm, heterosexuality is not simply an orientation among several, just one characteristic a person may have or lack in a neutrally-regarded field of options. It is the *presumed default*, and moreover, the central social arrangement around which all social relations are determined. Patrilineal property relations, ease of access to divorce and legal recourse in marriage, cultural pressures to procreate and 'continue the (father's) line', the patriarch as head of the nuclear or communal households—these are all institutions that arise from an enshrinement of heterosexuality, and furthermore entrench it as a *hierarchical, socio-economic* relation.

Crucially, the core insight here is that heterosexuality-as-regime is set up to extract domestic, sexual and reproductive labor from those deemed women under its logics. Its definition of womanhood and the narrowness of her stipulated role in society is oriented around *domestic confinement*, in rigorously naturalizing a positionality of abjection and servility towards others. In a very real sense, autonomous personhood itself is regarded as out of reach for women, as outside the domain to which they belong, a cruelty that is variously justified as done for women's own good, or a consequence of women's "true nature", their inward, subconscious, *biological* preference for their own subjugation. The fact that such subjugation must be ideologically, culturally, legally, economically, politically and violently forced upon women, often over their own vocalized or enacted objections, is never quite taken as contradicting this "natural" maxim.

We can see then why the regime of misogyny and heterosexualism needs must encompass such vast swathes of society, so that women can be reminded of their 'natural' inclination for servitude at every turn, as well as harshly punished if they ever unnaturally rebel against their biological nature. The strategies for domestic confinement throughout history have included legally preventing women from property-holding and earning an independent income, ostracizing and censuring spinsters and widows, denying women the franchise and the ability to hold office, and most reprehensibly solidifying forced marriage and rape as means of violent control. Some of the earliest laws punishing rape did not even consider the violated woman the wronged party—it was her husband or father owed recompense, due to the despoilment of his rightful property.

Broad as the scope of this already is, it is still insufficient to fully reckon with what it means for misogyny to be a cornerstone of society. Media itself is dominated by the perspective of men, created primarily by men for an audience that is largely presumed to be men as well. Their perspective is centered, cemented, elevated and enshrined while women continue to be *objectified*, to be depicted as prizes for (male) protagonists, as assets for a presumed-male lens, as objects to be appreciated aesthetically and owned by a suitable patriarch. Philosophers historically have extolled male virtues and deliberated on what makes a man a king, what makes him regal and stately, while categorizing women with beasts and animals and slaves, as synonymous with lesser beings of limited intellect and agency. Psychology and medicine have institutionalized and surgically mutilated women, whether for being insufficiently tame and docile or for being of the wrong race, dismissing their capacity for pain and anguish and advancing medicine on an edifice of their stacked bones and bodies. 'Woman' has not been just the bio-social category marked out as lesser, but synonymized with the base, the trivial, the surface-level, the unthinking, the eternally-enslaved counterpart to the liberated, leading, domineering, creative, intellectual Man.

Reckoning with the staggering totality of patriarchy, of misogyny as the very foundation of male-supremacist civilizations, can be disorienting and even incredibly debilitating. It is necessary, however, because it allows us to finally identify the core of its operation. The abjection of womanhood resides in the role carved out for women, in their being defined not just as the 'opposite' of men, but as fundamentally *deficient*, as representing a *lack*, bearing a *void* and a *nothingness* where men *are* and *have*. Biological difference becomes social construct, a tangible distinction elevated to *irreconcilable* identities. In doing so, 'woman' becomes everything 'man' isn't ... and also, everything 'man' *cannot be*. Everything 'man' *cannot sink to the level of*.

For that is the pernicious secret at the beating heart of every single regime:

how much energy and effort and sheer indoctrination is required to *enforce* and maintain it, to uphold its tenets and proscribe all deviation from them. Regimes require foot-soldiers, after all, enforcers willing to get their hands dirty in exchange for the wages of empire. Many a reign has been founded or toppled on the strength of its ideology, on the reasoning it was able to fashion to socially demarcate the enforcers from the serfs, on its ability to truly, sincerely blunt the capacity for empathy and make its valiant believe that they were materially above and distinct from those they crushed underfoot.

One could hardly ask for a more robust, enduring and ubiquitous ideology than misogyny, an all-pervasive system that we are inculcated into from the moment of our very birth. Our belief and investment in it often reflects the role assigned to us, and for men, whose supremacy, superiority and entitlement to sexual access and domestic labor is codified, even ensured by misogynistic doctrine, the investment is well worth the payoff. Thus, men do not only espouse and reproduce misogynistic belief, they *mandate* it as well, as much among each other as in their relationships and dealings with the women in their lives. They hold each other to misogynistic standards, to being adequately 'manly' in demeanor and execution, to eschewing genuine connection and love with women in favor of domination and the imposition of one's own will to whatever extent they can get away with. "Male bonding", touted almost as some manner of gendered sacrament, is in fact more akin to ritualistic violence, where men define themselves above and apart from the *weak*, the womanly. Any shortcoming in a man is attributed to the undue influence of a woman, whether an insufficiently-deferent partner or mother, or the manifestation of an intrinsic womanly emotion or quality that must be shaken off. The worst fate, met with censure, ostracism and outright violence, is being determined as *like them* in any way—whether that involves being too *empathetic* towards women, or too *similar* to them, too *effeminate* or *gay* or, even ...

This *enforced difference*, this strict social outlawing of actually-felt affinity between men and women on pain of exclusion, is hardly the exclusive domain of men. Women participate in it too, to varying degrees, because ultimately, to be raised in a misogynistic culture is to imbibe and internalize that which is described as a given, as the natural way things are. It is easy, in the absence of a widespread and rigorous feminist counterpoint, to say that *women* are shallow and banal and vapid and unintelligent, but *I*, personally, am not. Falling into the trap of distinguishing oneself as above the fray, an individual breaking the mold of derided womanhood, is a common and distressingly easy thing for many women and girls. It is a tactic that can, in the short term, yield dividends in approval and acceptance, since misogyny is a social currency that everyone bargains with, but in the final summation, no individual woman truly escapes the fate she is consigned to by dint of her gender, merely by participating in its denigration.

Despite this, some women never quite let go of exceptionalism, choosing to negotiate with patriarchal precepts on their own terms and making a grim sort of peace with patriarchal existence. The vast majority of conservative women are not in fact ignorant about patriarchy or their limited role in it, but have adopted a certain fatalistic attitude. To them, liberation from patriarchy is neither possible nor worth fighting for, as it would be no better than tilting at windmills. Better to accept that a woman is modest, domestic, a home-maker and child-rearer, and to perform according to those standards. In exchange, they receive the stability and security that a man who has claimed them can provide, a certain safety located within having to manage a single man's desires and needs. This 'traditional' life protects them, shelters them from the wider world which remains hostile and misogynistic, and is thus the 'smart' choice, one that all women ought to wisely and maturely accept.

Of course, such a bargain remains slanted in favor of the patriarch, and the task of satiating a single man's appetites is not quite as manageable as advertised. Leave aside the lack of true autonomy, the complete financial dependence, the everyday drudgery of domestic labor, and the lack of recourse in the (not infrequent) cases of abuse. The most glaring and evident pitfall is one that arises from straightforward patriarchal framing: that of the woman's value being entirely tied to her reproductive and sexual capacity. A woman who assents to the premises laid out by a patriarchal man is signing her own expiration date, affirming her own disposability and always dreading the day when she is no longer of use to her husband. She does and did everything right, from saving herself for marriage to comporting herself with dignity, but in spite of it all she is still only as valuable as her husband deems her, completely at his mercy. Her hopes are bound up entirely in the affection a patriarchal man might feel for a wife too old to excite him, a woman who mothered his children (but can bear him no more), and the slim chance that his eye does not wander to over to any younger woman willing to cut the same deal as she did.

The attitudes and logics described here form the foundation of an antifeminism that is primarily a traditionalist, reactionary fixation, but greatly informs the sexual politics of the liberal-left too. If you map the contours of the reactionary woman's worldview, you can arrive at the same conclusion many of them often do, led by a scarcity mindset and a fatalistic fear of having to zealously guard one's meager lot: that *other women*, far from being sisters, far from being fellow-travelers who can share burdens and pains, are in fact the *real enemy*. For if you have *somehow* successfully swindled yourself into believing that men are a prize, that legitimacy as a wife and mother is the greatest ambition permitted to you, that a man's approval—the apotheosis of which is the offer of marriage—is what makes or breaks a woman, then you have unwittingly entered yourself into a competition where other women are your opponents and your reward is patriarchal heterosexual existence.

(It's a miracle we've survived as long as we have).

Following this train of thought, we can see what shaped the emergence of *modesty* culture, of sex and sexual access becoming a fierce battleground among (heterosexual) women and men alike. In a field where women feel that they must actively compete for men, with sexual access to their bodies as their only leverage, a natural tension arises between those who consider it imperative that sexual relations occur only with the "safe", legally-enforced bounds of heterosexual marriage and those who do not see the point in doing so, who view marriage as more a shackle than a shield and who wish to embrace their sexuality more fully, instead of wielding it as a reward in a legal transaction.

Such dichotomy fosters resentment, breeds animosity, and imposes strict but contradictory standards on women, based on their sexual philosophies.

The domestic aspirants bitterly despise the sexually 'liberated', regarding them to be 'loose' women, 'floozies' and 'strumpets' whose inability to maintain a strict discipline devalues all women's sexual power and disincentivizes men from entering into marriages, since they can have their sexual needs met outside of the bounds of matrimony. It is almost trivial, in a way, to associate the sexually-liberated woman with a liberal, laissez-faire progressivism, one that rejects the stuffy, confining, almost *backwards* outlook of the 'modest' woman. The sexually-liberated woman, so the myth tells, is a woman who is in charge of her *own* sexual destiny, who determines access to her body on her own terms and isn't afraid to enjoy sex, to actively seek it out, even! Is it any wonder, then, that she was able to single-handedly overthrow patriarchy, chipping away at its stalwart edifices one orgasm at a time?

Perhaps this is a disappointing revelation to some readers, but based on our current socio-political circumstances, free love and sexual liberation did not in fact succeed in lighting women's way to equality and emancipation. It has been tried more than once, the pendulum swinging inexorably between 'whore' and 'madonna', cycling them in and out of vogue, but ultimately liberating sex without liberating women rarely seems to achieve the desired outcomes. As much as men love sexually-liberated women—love sleeping with them without strings attached most of all—eventually it comes time to settle down, time to return to the patriarchal fold, at which point he's back to searching for his perfect, virginal, *modest* woman. As it so happens, in order to be liberated, women don't *just* need the freedom to sleep with anyone of their choosing, but also require the ability to earn, inherit, purchase property, influence policy—you know, *liberation*, the ability to exist independently of men. Otherwise, they are merely trying to negotiate between two tightropes: being the matronly madonna without being too prudish or dull, or being the sexually-liberated free lover without also being considered disposable, tainted, or *too* into sex, all things that deny her the status of "wife material".

Which brings us to the final, cruel joke of the farce that is patriarchy and the misogyny that empowers it. This force that pervades all legal, socio-economic, and political institutions, that structures the atomic family unit itself, and that seeps into our most private intimate moments also, ultimately, robs most of us of the capacity for the kind of intimacy we crave. The patriarchal man may covet the sexually free woman to bed and may wish to trot out the modest woman at family gatherings, but he never quite manages to respect either. Cherish, perhaps, prize as a conquest or a tamed servant, even, but true, actual respect, the appreciation one engenders for a fellow person's wit and charm and intellect and compassion and genuine, sparkling insight—why, *that* kind of admiration, that kind of *love*, is only reserved for fellow men.

Because misogyny is an un-personing of the woman, a dictum to hold her in contempt, to slander everything associated with her, and burn away one's ability to empathize with her state. She is only as good to you as the function she can serve, whether helpmeet or matron or just a good fuck. If one is to humanize her, it requires tearing the veil misogyny places over all our eyes and reckoning with the codified strictures of patriarchy in fact and in execution. To truly, actually love her, you must begin to dismantle everything you've been raised to believe about her.

Let me assure you, reader: I love women with all I am and all I can be, and I hope that you do too, or will in time.

# "Heterosexuality is a Regime": On the Coercive Nature of Patriarchy

How do politics affect attraction?

This question might strike one as absurd, since on the most basic, bio-physiological level, attraction is simply an internal chemical process, a set of feelings, emotions, and bodily responses to another individual that, altogether, comprise our experiences of desire, intimacy, perhaps even romance. There is a sense in which attraction, unique and personal and individualized as it is, is thought to be *beyond* politics, beyond the realm of the social, an innate, internal experience untouched by external influence. Suggestions to the contrary can, in fact, take a particularly charged turn, especially when there exist well-funded and highly-motivated reactionary cohorts whose ideological obsession is the eradication of queer attraction and queer modes of existence.

Still, it is naive to presume that our circumstances, environments, and the social forces that govern them have *no* relationship to our attraction—especially when it comes to how we choose to *express* or *repress* it. The attraction we feel may be internal and personal, but how we act on that attraction is a social matter, one that holds differing ramifications for us based on identity, based on whether we are of the demographic permitted sexual autonomy, or one of the *Others*.

Not all attractions are equal under the heterosexual regime, after all.

There is a temptation to simplify the discussion by highlighting how heterosexuality is *naturalized*, is considered the only permissible sexuality under patriarchy, but even that much is an overstatement. Women, in some sense, have *no* permissible sexuality and have never been granted the license or liberty to express and embody any attraction, even to men. The reduction of women to sexual chattel and men's property sharply limits their agency in all matters, especially sexual. In a sense, women who express any degree of sexuality have always been seen as *deviant*, as exhibiting a behavior and aspiring to a freedom that only men have had a right to claim. A woman's sexuality, before anything else, is thus to be *tamed, domesticated, confined* as much as she herself is, a force that must never be allowed to spiral out of control and must always be subject to the whims and commands of the men who own her, whether father, brother, husband or any other proximal patriarch with dominion over her.

*Modesty politics* emerged out of this imperative to police women's sexuality, a set of social norms and customs that provides justification and ensures consequences for misbehavior. Women are constantly reminded that their worth is entirely bound up in how many and *which* men they permit sexual access to their body, making expressions of attraction—leave alone actual *intercourse*—an act that demeans, degrades, and devalues them. The project of women's objectification and reduction to property, to sexual resources, is thoroughly subsumed even into matters of social custom and internalized by women themselves, as they are forced to navigate the maze of men's desires. Women are frequently held responsible for how others perceive them, whether too frigid or too promiscuous, whether they rebuff men's advances (and are thereby chastised for rejecting those who have more of a claim to their bodies than they do), or whether they accept and are consequently denigrated as *easy, promiscuous* and *sullied* in some indelible way. Marriage, the sole institution through which women are granted any degree of status or respect, then becomes an arbiter of respectability, by elevating those who become privatized reproductive assets and further patrilineality. This mean prize, a slightly more gilded cage than the alternative, is leveraged to keep women in line and ensure complicity with the heterosexual regime.

Keeping this in mind, and observing the historical suppression of women's sexuality, it is perhaps not a surprise that much of women's liberation has focused on the act of liberating sexuality, on securing women's right to freely express their desires in the manner men have for centuries. While men are venerated for their virility, for successfully pursuing women and demonstrating their status via desirability, women are punished for similar behaviors. Desirability reinforces the mythology of a man and lessens the status of a woman; surely, achieving parity in this regard would be a crucial component of the feminist struggle.

Therein lies a crucial blunder, however, one that has been made repeatedly despite repeated failure. While it is true that a woman's *respectability* may depend upon the rigid subjugation and control of her sexuality, that does not necessarily mean that simply expressing sexual desire and attempting to exercise sexual autonomy furthers women's cause. For there have always been women for whom libidinous behavior is permissible—encouraged, even—women who have always been in demand, who have served the purpose of being sexually available to men whose social rituals hinge upon the performance of sexuality as conquest, as violence, as an exercise of manhood's inherent sexual freedom. They have simply been women who were considered *public property* rather than private, marginalized women who are denied even the barest protection of the patriarchal bargain. Many relations of power are interwoven with (hetero)sexuality, cleaving differences between *private* and *public* women, between women you "take home to the parents" and women whose very identity marks them as lesser, as fit for little more than being consumed and then discarded by men. This stigma around women and sexuality is not one that vanishes by willing it so, and has in fact persisted to the modern day, against the backdrop of the fight for women's rights.

This is the bedrock of heterosexuality as a regime: one where women are supposed to submit to men's sexuality and men's desire to possess them and bear all the consequences for that desire, whether reproductive, social, or economic. In that sense, 'heterosexuality' is not so much something women are *rewarded* for acquiescing to, but simply an expectation and a duty they must fulfill, the rejection of which incurs additional consequences over and above the misogynistic subordination of womanhood.

Knowing this, it is little wonder that queer women are so frequently coerced into negotiating their sexualities and identities with a society that fundamentally wants to stamp out any possibility of women rejecting men. Women existing independent of men is often made socioeconomically untenable, whether it's limitations on income, property-holding, or the basic ability to open an account without a husband's permission, or familial and community ostracism for failing to marry a man by a certain age. In those cultures where the patriarchal contradictions are particularly harsh, the consequences may be more straightforwardly violent and directly coercive, with many a woman, irrespective of identity, subject to forced marriage in the event she fails to comply with her family's wishes.

Discussions of 'heterosexuality' therefore cannot occur in a neutral context, as though our whole society is not organized around the violent enforcement of women's status as male property. Women are subject to violence both within the home and without, provided a patriarchal bargain that puts Faustian ones to shame: whether to accept one's lot as a domesticized indentured servant and saddled with the bulk of childcare, domestic work, *and* sexual labor, or to reject this heterosexualist imperative and incur the wrath of entire communities. Will you accept a slow, monotonous, banal death, crushed under the weight of gestation and repetitive, unrewarding ardor, or will you allow yourself to be an acceptable target of abuse by all, having repudiated a woman's only role and function under patriarchy? This is a choice whose final, punctuated cruelty is simply that getting to make the choice is itself considered kindness, for there exist classes of women who are implicitly sorted into the latter category without getting to make the choice at all.

No conversation about patriarchy, misogyny, feminism, or sexuality can be had without this crucial context, without acknowledging how much of a hollow choice the patriarchal bargain is. The *freedom to choose* is no freedom at all when every option is a cage, just a different degree of oppression rather than actual, authentic emancipation. The true test of freedom is in asking whether one has the freedom to walk away, to reject an offer without consequence, to pull the plug without being punished for it. The heterosexual regime will stand tall for as long as a woman's safety and prosperity are contingent on male ownership. Until women can embrace an autonomous existence outside of the domestic sphere, outside of patriarchal, androcentric existence without facing violent correction, we are not free.

Heterosexuality is a regime, and like every unjust regime, it too will be abolished.

# Understanding Transmisogyny, Part Two: Homophobia and Transphobia

What is it like to grow up in a heterosexualist world when you aren't heterosexual?

'Understanding Transmisogyny, Part One' was somewhat abstract in its discussion of the culture of heterosexualism, speaking of patriarchy and its engendering misogyny as an omnipresent social substrate, one that we are all immersed in and unable to disentangle our selves, our consciousnesses and our experiences from. In this one, let's attempt to be more explicit about that process of osmosis, of developing, imbibing and reacting to the perpetual reinforcement of the patriarchal society.

We've established how it can already be damaging and abusive to internalize the precepts of a patriarchal society even when you *are* heterosexual. Children, by dint of being dependents, wards and constantly-learning minds, navigate a world where even if adults do not consciously sit down and explain the nuances of gender to them, they are still exposed to gendered messaging and gendered realms as a matter of course. Teachers expect girls to do less well at mathematical and scientific subjects, a discouragement they pick up on even when the cues are subtle. Boys are given more of a license to be loud, disruptive, boisterous and to 'misbehave' in ways girls are more stringently punished for or prevented from doing. Thus, by a simple process of feeling out the bounds of the permissible and impermissible, as all children are wont to do, they grow up feeling the restrictions and borders placed around them by their presumed gender, even if they cannot name it as such.

Of course, this does not necessarily mean that every child accepts their lot, is content with what they are permitted and never strays from what is allowed of them. Children test all these boundaries to different degrees, receive different degrees of backlash and punitive responses and variously resolve to conform or rebel in their own, particular ways. Social teachings are not a simple matter of one's childhood indoctrination taking root and indelibly dictating their attitudes, actions and beliefs for the rest of their lives, else we'd all be staunch patriarchs and deferential helpmeets, perfectly cleaved along the lines of sex assigned at birth. In our own ways, we steal away and hide the parts of ourselves we are told we cannot express, that we learn we must guard jealously until the time comes when we can be free.

These observations of acculturation are the core of *socialization theory*, a theory that aims to explicate the manner in which a culture reproduces itself. A key insight here would be that there are many different *vectors* for this socialization, many of them distinct, if not mutually exclusive: *class* for example is a critical determiner of how one relates to authority and oppression, whether one grew up internalizing their own disposability or their own inherent worth, based on family wealth. Therefore, while this can account for a certain degree of consistency in belief and behavior, determined by a person's various vectors of socialization, the kinds of socialization one experiences themselves vary immensely, across one's various identities. In fact, the singular common thread through this staggering variety of socializations remains that cross-cultural, near-universal maxim: misogyny itself.

That is to say, the constant that cuts across cultures is that we are all *socialized misogynistic*.

We see this acutely in the way heterosexualism operates and how women, rather than forming a collective consciousness based on their shared suffering, locate their value in their *domestic worth* or *sexual availability* to men. This is something that is internalized early, quickly and without necessarily being explicitly stated, but still lived nonetheless. It is not merely that 'man' and 'woman' are constructed as mutually exclusive categories, but also that women are expected to submit and be deferential, naturalizing what is ultimately a labor relation of sexual, domestic and reproductive extractivism. This internalization of misogynistic precepts also functions as a *false consciousness*, a form of identification with the *oppressor's view* of oneself that prevents the subjugated from self-actualizing and forming solidarity against their own oppression.

Women thus have a great deal to contend with in their socialization and a great many hazards in coming to terms with it. Some dissociate from womanhood by idealizing themselves as exceptions to the misogynistic norm, while others fatalistically accept patriarchal bargains and seek to content themselves with their own mean spheres of influence. Others still attempt to navigate male-dominated spheres by emulating male social dynamics— wearing suits, deepening their voices, obeying certain contradictory standards of requirements of femininity and masculine projection as best they can—to varying degrees of success. In all these cases, there's a certain *negotiation* or *compromise* with misogynistic social doctrines, a desire to mitigate them as best one can and still tolerate one's everyday existence.

So what is done to those who *cannot* compromise? If navigating heterosexualism as a heterosexual is so painful, how do those who *aren't* fare?

Not well.

An important, implicit aspect of misogynistic socialization is that it carries with it an unspoken edict of *mandatory* heterosexuality. There is not, at any point in a woman's life, an interrogation of her own desires, her own sexuality or identity as something that can exist independent of men and men's desires. Whether she is a lesbian, an asexual, a bisexual who prefers women or even a heterosexual woman who doesn't favor a particular man—her own feelings, opinions and wants in the matter are considered secondary to those of the man trying to claim her. Irrespective of the particulars of the woman's condition, a forced marriage will go through, a sexual assault will be rationalized and forgiven, rejection will be demonized, frigidity punished and a man's claim over her body and subjugated labor held paramount over her own claim to autonomy, to personhood. To be *woman* means to be *men's*, to be consigned to the ownership of another at the very moment of birth.

Not only is this true in adulthood, it is the context that informs and shapes all of girlhood as well. Many cultures do not even consider lesbianism as extant, or have a word to describe it, because everything a woman *is* or is meant to be is oriented around male ownership. Some go so far as to deny the possibility of romance and sexuality between women as *possible at all*, describing such emotions between women as intense kinship and even 'natural' in its own right, as a 'precursor' or 'practice' for true, heterosexual romance after 'maturity'. Lesbianism thus is both erased and infantilized, subsumed into the homoerotic realm of women's friendship, solidifying the inability of women to be in sexual relationships with each other by reinforcing the inability of a woman to *claim* another; they are both considered *unclaimed* by men-in-waiting.

Despite these barriers both cultural and conceptual, where women who defy heterosexuality are granted the burden of having to imagine such an existence from whole cloth, women *have* managed to exist with each other and outside the prying claws of men's ownership. Such existences, once actuated, have also been harshly punished if discovered and expunged from the historical record as part of the effort to keeping it obscured, unnamed, and out of the realm of the real.

Rape is a tool often deployed to mandate patriarchal compliance, and I think we need not linger more on the topic. Readers may find some value in punching a nearby cushion and then continuing.

Given the impossibility of existing autonomously as a woman historically, it is perhaps no surprise that people faced with the prospect of their biology consigning them to a lifetime of reproductive and sexual servitude did in many instances resort to masking their gender as best as they could manage. In the absence of modern medical advancements such as hormone replacement therapy, it is unclear whether any particular instance of cross-dressing can conclusively be regarded a trans man or a butch lesbian, especially given that such delineations were not as explicit historically (though of course in some cases, we have the individuals' own recorded thoughts on the matter of how they would prefer to be regarded even privately, which clarifies the issue somewhat). What we can conclusively say is that even prior to the possibility of medical intervention, individuals have attempted to *transcend* their biodestiny and leave behind the fetters of womanhood, whether by garb or demeanor, though of course very few were given the opportunity to even make the attempt.

We can thus see that in aggregate, regardless of how those marked for womanhood at birth attempt to dissociate from the most pernicious aspects of that marking, whether they are heterosexuals who seek a modicum of independence or lesbians who seek a total break from gendering and androcentric existence, patriarchy intends to confine and repurpose them all to their singular permitted role under its violent regime, that of the *reproducer*, the *birther*, the *broodmare*, the doting wife, nurturing mother, subjugated woman. This is the totalizing violence that Adrienne Rich called *compulsory heterosexuality*, the imperative embedded into everything from our cultural messaging to socio-economic structures. The identity of the individual and their self-actualization becomes irrelevant: straight, bi, lesbian, ace, non-binary, trans, none of it matters to the patriarchal order. Whether such an individual has a uterus or not, is even capable of bearing children or not, the logics still apply and their existence is still collapsed into the forced labor of womanhood, the caring for all others besides themselves.

Additionally, this remains the biggest axis of delegitimization and oppression for trans men well into the modern era. The dearth of research in the sphere of reproductive health juts painfully into trans men's healthcare as well, compounding the issue of insufficient research into trans people's bodies with the thorough, inescapable gendering of all reproductive and natal care. When every aspect of medicine related to the uterus is gated off as "women's health", trans men face constant reminders from both the field and the staff inhabiting it that their gendered past will always haunt them. Hysterectomies are difficult to acquire and guidance for those who do want to bear children is sparse, making every aspect of navigating this feminized labyrinth a thoroughly gendered nightmare.

Homophobia and transphobia towards those coerced into the category of the 'female sex' is, in every particularity, undergirded by the general principle of *treating the 'lapsed woman' like a potential womb to reclaim*. 'Woman's' social construction strives to orient her towards this singular purpose, prunes every other possibility from the branching paths of her life, and tallies up the sum of her worth as nothing more or less than her ability to birth. Should a woman fail this singular imperative, should she fall short of the respectable ideal of male-owned broodmare, she becomes something ... lesser. Something more abject than abject, reviled on top of being subjugated, her entire being subsumed into the conceptualized fallowness of bad soil, the charred and lifeless expanses of inhospitable wastes ... *barren*. She becomes, in a sense, reduced to a subset of a subset, more incomplete than even the incomplete man that is 'woman', morphing into a thing that only has sexual worth, a servile robot that is only as good as the labor—sexual, domestic, uncompensated, unvalorized—that can be extracted from her. Every nominal protection that being a man's private property could possibly extend to her is forever revoked unless she can somehow grovel sufficiently to make up for her gestational deficiencies.

Readers might do well to put a pin in this paragraph, to keep it in the back of their minds. We'll have to return to it later.

Thorough as this regime is with regards to its colonized subjects, one aspect we must also contend with is the regime's enforcers, those who deploy its violences most regularly and seek to extract the most benefits from upholding it. As it so happens, the wages of patriarchy are not always sufficient to keep its strongest soldiers in line, necessitating the use of lateral as well as vertical violence to maintain order, with desertion meriting particularly severe disciplinary action. For compulsory heterosexuality is a regulation that even men are expected to honor, and even though we do not often conceptualize it as 'constraining' men in the same way, given that they are the ones extracting reproductive value from the patriarchal subjects they oversee, in some cases, it makes sense to do so—such as the cases where they do not desire the role of warden over a woman's autonomy at all.

A fascinating quirk of a misogynistic society is how well it lends itself to homoeroticism, to the reserving of men's admiration, camaraderie, adoration, respect, affection, and in some senses, *love*, solely for other men. The depersonalization of women, the denial of their capacity to think and feel 'on the same level' as the elevated, intellectual, reasoning, and ideating Man, also gates the ability for men to truly empathize and engage with women as they do with other men. Men romanticize other men, romanticize the notion of brotherhood and comradeship with their male companions, often ritualized in violent institutions such as the military, or rooted in the petty interpersonal violences of hazing, roughhousing, of being intimate with blood and sweat if not spit and cum. It is only logical, consequential—natural, even—for some men to take this innate homoeroticism of misogynistic society to its natural conclusion.

Patriarchy, however, as male-supremacist as it may be, is ultimately founded on *reproductive* logics. Men may love other men but they *must* fuck women, must maintain and naturalize the patriarchal order, or else risk exposing the farce. Some may still find some refuge in masculinity, in the aesthetics and performance of maleness even while abandoning the function, and indeed some societies have allowed men to retain their male *essence* so long as they could still be *men*, still abhor femininity and maintain the social boundary between themselves and essentialized 'womanhood'. Of course, this has necessitated that their *counterpart* be 'unmanned' instead, having the proximity to 'womanhood' quite literally *thrust* upon them, upholding the gendering of intercourse itself and patriarchy's blunt, forceful, violent conceptions of sexual relations between two people. If one is, fairly, moved to object that homosexual relations could never mirror heterosexualism, one might have to consider that the nomenclature of *top* and *bottom* with regard to sexual roles is perhaps unintentionally revealing in that regard.

Such an unmanned man is a deserter, an aberration that has more wholly given up his claim to manhood's core tenets, one whose state illustrates a core truth about patriarchal gender construction: that gender has *verticality* but not *upward mobility*. Gendered oppression can be intensified but hardly ever alleviated, an ordinance to execute that can be failed in many ways. While the rubric of gendered performance can and has shifted with time and culture, it has also always been narrowly-defined, with definitions particularly prone to *contraction* in reactionary times. There have been times when *all* homosexual men have been unmanned, and no periods where none of them were.

Patriarchy, then, is akin to the most stringent of regimes, the harshest of occupations, rigorously segregating citizen from slave on pain of treason. It is much easier to be cast out of its citadels than it is to breach the walls of the metropole, easier to have one's citizenship revoked than to find a feasible path to naturalization. This is the terror that lurks at the heart of every imperial citizen, every settler on contested lands: the conditionality of their status, which is dependent entirely on how strenuously they fight for their flag. No matter how aggrandizing patriarchy is, no matter how jealously it reserves the qualities of true intellect, valor, strength, virility, and sovereignty for men, those are also standards that can be fallen short of and cease applying to a man at the barest suspicion of inadequate ideological fealty.

That is what it truly means for gender to be *socially constructed*, for our gendered behaviors to be socialized and taught and constantly graded. The gender conservative would have you believe that this is a natural system, a mundane and banal and even drolly simplistic one, blunt in the way all conservative ideals tend to be: a mere division of humanity into 'man' and 'woman' based on trivially-observed sex characteristics, an uncontested binary of human expression and existence. While I do not disagree that there is a binary that lurks at the heart of gender relations, it is very much not a biologically-ordained one.

It is not rooted in the vulgar materialism of a finite set of sexed features, but in the ideological determinants of who is allowed to be master of their own destiny and who must be indentured to them, who is deemed to have worth and who is deemed to be worthless. It is about loyalty to a regime, participation in its everyday violence, conformity to its edicts, and unwavering belief in its glory. The binary is one of colonizer and colonized, of naturalized and second-class citizen, of the honored subject and the reviled object.

The binary is the socially constructed division between who is considered human, and who is not.

Gender, or *gendering*, rather, can itself be considered a process of violence, a process that is innately othering, dehumanizing, and *lessening*. 'Man' and 'mankind' are deployed often as synonymous with humanity, with human existence, not because 'man' is considered the 'default' state of a human, but the *only* state, the only state that matters. 'Man' and 'human' are synonyms;

'human' and 'woman' are arguably antagonistically defined. To gender a person is to un-person them, to make them something lesser than a man, whether that's potential male property or a failed example of manhood, a state that no person would ever wish to be reduced to.

... Though of course, that begs the question.

What if someone did?

It defies all sense, does it not? Logically, one can see clearly why some lesbians and gay and trans men have historically donned the cloak of masculinity, have attempted to shield themselves from the gendering process by emulating those not subjected to it. No one, *no person* would ever dream of doing the inverse, of emulating the abject, of actually, actively, *sincerely* trying to be a woman. It goes against all reason, all common patriarchal understanding! Why would anyone attempt to inhabit the positionality of the degraded, occupy the position of the derided, willingly cast themselves down from the upper echelons of the castes to cavort about as one of the untouchables? It is profane, it is BLASPHEMY, it is *PERVERSE* and **VULGAR** and **UNNATURAL!!!!**

NO ONE, no *thing* that can be considered a reasonable, sane person, a thinking, intelligent being worthy of being considered human, would ever do such a thing.

And if they did?

If they DARED to?

They would be dealt with. Oh, they would *have* to be dealt with.

# Understanding Transmisogyny, Part Three: Constructing the Transsexual

Do boys experience gendered violence?

We left the previous chapter talking about *gendering* as a process, as an action that takes the autonomous human and *reduces* his autonomy, *lessens* his status and *subjugates* him under the gendered regime. The principal mode by which this is done is through *sexing*, the social process of gendering the body, whereby certain anatomical features in aggregate are granted outsized social meaning and determine one's social standing, primarily (though not exhaustively) by means of their relation to gestational capacity. Those sorted into the category burdened with reproductive, domestic and sexual labor—women—are dehumanized and denied full personhood. Furthermore, *heterosexualist* logics can position someone closer to or further away from the abject woman, whereby any violation of patriarchy's organization around its own reproduction carries a commensurate sentence. Men are thus positioned as the beneficiaries of an extractive labor relation, one that they must enforce and uphold to continue reaping its rewards.

Though of course, this begs the question: how does one become a man? How is one prepared and trained for a lifetime of serving the regime?

Recalling the verticality of the gendered hierarchy, we understand how much easier it is to become more 'like' a woman than a man, to have one's humanity denied than built up, to fall further down the ladder than to ascend its rungs. This manner of conceptualizing patriarchy and its enabling misogyny makes one very important elision, however: it does not quite account for children.

No child is a man or a woman, of course, and for a time, determining what a child's sex might be is a difficult prospect by sight alone, requiring parents to resort to fairly explicit external gendered markers in order to distinguish which sex-caste their progeny has been sorted into. The realm of gender and sexuality is largely placed out of reach of children, though the boundary is far more porous than it perhaps should be and frequently trickles down to shape and mold their social development. Children are enmeshed in a process of perpetual *becoming*, much like we all are, only more explicitly so. They are *socialized* into various roles according to class, race, sex, ability, and more, their existence defined and determined by the authority of others, their world divided into what they are *allowed* to be and what they must never become. Girls quickly learn just how rigidly-bounded their worlds are, how narrowly their expected selves are defined. Boys in turn quickly pick up how much they *can* be, intuit how much possibility is afforded them even when it is very little, and implicitly understand that their own worlds are not permitted to overlap with that of the girls.

Except for the boys who don't.

Rules and edicts only go so far, after all, and for all of history, children have always known better than their betters, no matter how much their parents have insisted that they don't. Not every punishment stings enough to dissuade, not every rebuke inspires compliance and not every child grows into the adult that their guardians so desperately wanted them to be. We know that there are girls who, despite being told that kisses are for boys, steal them from each other's lips behind closed doors and whispered glances, who think fondly of the boots and carabiners they'll sport when they're older. Similarly, there are boys for whom the reproachments don't ... *stick*.

Violence is, of course, a gendering process.

Which is to say that violence is also thoroughly *gendered*, an act that connotes certain delineations in a world where aggression, strength and *power* are all considered the domain of men, while women are meant to—for various meanings of this phrase—*take it*. There is thus a terrible anxiety that centers upon the boy, this creature that is destined to grow up and become a man with all the power and vigor and virility that embodies, but is not quite a man *yet*, is distressingly proximate to the reviled woman by dint of his dependence and relative frailty and subjection to authority. For all the arrogant assertions of the naturalness of gender, most cultures have understood that boys need to be *made* men, need to be inculcated and indoctrinated into the cult that is manhood, and many have accordingly acknowledged this explicitly via the coming-of-age, the rituals and processes through which a pitiable boy, this child that is a potential-man, can demonstrate his readiness for the mantle and harshly divide his boyhood from manhood, demonstrating definitively that he has successfully left his juvenile weakness behind him.

Though of course, this begs the question: what of those who do not succeed?

If you can succeed in overcoming boyhood to become a man, what happens if you *fail*?

Paradoxically, boys are often subjected to violence to make them men, are broken down and further abjected in a bid to make them reject that abjection. A boy that is not sufficiently aggressive is made the subject of aggression, a boy that feels too much is angrily taught that the only feeling he can express safely is anger, and a boy that refuses to prey on others is brutally made to understand that that will mark *him* as prey himself. Boys have to like girls without loving them, without wanting to be like them or among them. Boys have to reserve affection and admiration and camaraderie for other boys, without crossing the threshold that makes that affection too much like the affection only a girl can harbor for a boy. Boys have to prepare to be men, and any insufficiency in that regard must be violently corrected until the boy decides that doling out the beatings is better than being on the receiving end.

Still, some boys never quite learn what's good for them.

There is another purpose to this omnipresent violent *correction*, this repeated attempted breaking of the boy to reveal the putative man ensconced within, irrespective of how old the arrested boy actually gets. Simply put, should the constant testing of manhood be too agonizing, the repeated failure to become that which the boy was supposed to become too much to bear, and the torturous excesses of others' brotherhood too exclusionary and ostracizing, then the failed man, the persevering boy, can finally elect to stop persevering, one way if not another, thereby ridding the world of his malodorous taint.

Proving rituals never quite ceased, after all, even if they have become somewhat more esoteric and less momentous.

So far the experiences described herein could apply to people of quite a few identities, generalized as they are to 'boy who does not perform masculinity appropriately'. The sources of this inadequacy can even be located outside of a gendered paradigm (such as along racial or religious lines, for example) given how synonymous demeaning a man is with gendering him, how the worst insults that can be levied at a man or type of man involve likening him to a type of woman. Even so, the sharpest disciplining is reserved for those boys who show signs that they are unlikely to ever be man enough, who do not love or fuck or *be* in the manner a man ought to. For the single worst outcome possible, the result that must be avoided at all costs, is absolutely untenable in a male-supremacist society.

Namely: What if the boy is neither broken nor discouraged by the disciplining, and perseveres without becoming a man?

What if a boy, despite being shown exactly what will be done to him for rejecting his biodetermined destiny, chooses it anyway?

What if a boy actually chooses to be a woman?

No regime can afford to take desertion lightly, but outright treason, actual and legitimate identification with the occupied, the exploited—that it cannot countenance under *any* circumstance. If one's entire ideology is built on a myth of essentialized superiority, of a difference between the master and the slave that is innate and natural and impossible to transcend, then legitimizing any porosity between the two contradictory categories, permitting any identification of the humane Self with the dehumanized Other, *has* to be treated as an existential threat, a possible catastrophe in the making. Traitors to the regime need to be sought out and suppressed with all possible zeal, every last one stamped out and marginalized to the utter fringes.

Which all, ultimately, amounts to this: if society ever erroneously constructs a transsexual, she needs to be immediately, instantly destroyed.

There is a rich irony inherent to this destruction, however, which is that in attempting to destroy the transsexual, patriarchal society actually constructs her. For in a society that genders everything, every mechanism, essence, and feature, the act of violently negating the transsexual's potential manhood, of casting her out from the upper echelons of the humanized down to the depths of the untouchables, is an act inseparable from the misogynistic processes by which all besides the patriarchal man are ultimately defined. Creation in destruction, construction by nullification, patriarchy births its own antithesis in hatred, by expelling its worst traitors for the unforgivable sin of seeing worth in all that it did not want them to be.

As it so happens, under patriarchal ideology, womanhood is the worst fate that a person can be consigned to.

We can now truly begin to ascertain the shape that transmisogyny materially takes, finally begin to put the pieces together after reckoning with gender as a socially-constructed regime of dehumanization predicated on specific forms of labor extraction. The failure to take up the mantle of manhood, or the temerity to wilfully reject it carries the penalty of reassignment, of revocation of any and all respectability that existence under patriarchal gender affords. The transsexual, having already failed at being a man, is relegated to the simultaneous state of failed woman as well, given her inability to serve patriarchy's reproductive logics, to become a somewhat valued property utilized to perpetuate patrilineality. Her exploitation takes an acutely sexual form, her purpose defined and distilled into the sole function that women are reduced to if (and when) they cannot bear a man's children.

Despite this reduction of the transsexual's existence to her sexual availability, she is also peculiarly denied something crucial: *recognition*. While it may be permissible to treat the transsexual like a woman, to degrade her and objectify her and sexualize her as one, she cannot at any point be *named* as one, cannot be admitted to have achieved the status that those who violate her implicitly categorize her into even as they commit the violation. No, the transsexual has to be something else, has to be the boy who could never grow up, the sissy who couldn't be manly enough, or the homosexual whose lust for straight men drove her to self-mutilation. In order for her to be the ur-example of dehumanization, the totalized non-person that exists in the harshest contrast against the Natural Man, she must be hurled out of gendered classification so utterly that she becomes Something Else, held up as a degendered freak even as she is subjected to the full force of gendering.

In this sense the transsexual and her body become the site upon which any and every patriarchal excess can be enacted without remorse, the brutalized Other who is not simply a colonized subject of the regime, but a barbarian milling at the gates, at once wretched and pitiable while also representing the crisis that could undo the regime's very foundations. All regimes sooner or later need an external threat to divert attention to, a foreign enemy for its people to focus on so that the extant tyranny seems preferable, even tame by comparison, and the transsexual is the Gendered Empire's own Vandal. She is the menace against whom any violence can be justified, both the failed man who can be beaten senseless and the failed woman who can be raped with impunity, against whom no amount of harm is unjustifiable.

Speaking in plain terms, the tranny is constructed as the union of fag and whore.

What, then, is *transmisogyny*? It is the process by which those conscripted into the male sex under patriarchy are denaturalized and dehumanized, being demoted from potentially liberated agent to subjugated object. It is the intensification of misogyny in a manner that does not merely enforce sexual difference but explicitly penalizes the failure to uphold it. It is the *degendering* of the male subject, enacted to reconstruct her into an unperson who cannot be considered to be wronged, violated, or otherwise harmed, upon whom sexual exploitation and feminized labor extraction can be enacted with impunity. More broadly, if misogyny is the force that elevates men at the expense of women, then transmisogyny is the complementary force that makes examples out of those who dare to turn their backs on the resulting gendered rewards. Transmisogyny is the reminder, the warning, the deterrent: "Be the man you were meant to be, *or else.*"

# II

# Part Two: Lesbian Feminism

*Lesbian feminism has been the school of thought that has most markedly impacted me and how I see the world. Here, I do my best to incorporate its observations into a modern transfeminist framework.*

# Understanding Lesbophobia, Part One: Diabolus ex Machina

## Monstress

In *Right Wing Women*, Andrea Dworkin discusses her experience at the National Women's Conference in 1977. She talked about how the conservative women present spoke to her animatedly about lesbians all being rapists. A liberal, Black delegate from Texas confessed to Dworkin that the local white women from her town had assured her that a 'personally filthy' lesbian would call her dirty names and assault her at the conference. Dworkin then details how, despite admitting that they had not personally heard of any cases of lesbians assaulting women, despite knowing that their daughters were more likely to be harmed by a man within their families than a lesbian they did not know and had never heard of, the monstrosity of the lesbian, her abominable, external, downright demonic sexual threat to the family still featured more prominently in their minds. Male violence under heterosexuality is a routine matter, after all, everyday to the point of being banal. The specter of the lesbian, however, is a much more alarming and evocative threat—unlike a man, a lesbian is a threat to the *family*.

This brings us to a natural, almost inevitable question, one that certainly everyone has considered in their lives: are lesbians *privileged*?

One of the foremost radical feminist minds of our time, James Somerton, in his original and groundbreaking video *Reclaiming the 'Q' Word*, discusses the obscenity case brought against lesbian author Radclyffe Hall to illustrate this seemingly contradictory social phenomenon. James Douglas, a male critic, charged that Hall's *Well of Loneliness* was "immoral propaganda", writing that he "would rather give a healthy boy or a healthy girl a phial of prussic acid than this novel". Of course, such a case presented a rather thorny issue to the English gentlemen in charge of the courts at the time—namely, the daunting task of attempting to convict Hall without ever once mentioning 'lesbianism', a taboo subject that they were hesitant to even name publicly. Unable to find a reasonable legal strategy that could skirt around this thorny roadblock, the case against Hall was summarily dismissed, allowing her to simply "carry on in her happy life", per Somerton.

Well, except—that's not quite what happened, at least not outside the fevered imaginings of a gay man cosplaying as a YouTuber. What did in fact happen was that Hall's publisher put out a call to potential witnesses who might be willing to stand against the book's censorship, most of whom never responded. Hall lost the obscenity case itself and the subsequent appeal, which resulted in an order to destroy all copies of the book in the United Kingdom. This is a fact bluntly and accessibly stated without much ambiguity on the author's Wikipedia page, compelling one to marvel at how exactly a person speaking about this case could possibly misconstrue the result so utterly. Here, the lie itself is not so interesting as the various possible motives behind it, the thought processes that might lead a gay man—supposedly in community with lesbians, that first letter in the 'LGBT' acronym—to try to portray a historical reality that would allow a lesbian to walk away unmolested after an encounter with the law.

If there's one thing that Somerton managed to convey accurately despite his best efforts, it is the response that a heterosexualist society has towards lesbianism as a concept. Befuddlement, discomfort and denial pervade the cultural attitudes towards the idea of women being able to love other women romantically, an unsettled reaction undergirded by a certain dread, an uncanny feeling that something has gone deeply, terribly wrong. It is the bone-suffusing terror of encountering something that *cannot be*, that *should not be*, that unholy, monstrous shadow whose name can scarcely be spoken in polite company, lest its evil gaze be cast upon all present.

That unnamability is palpable in *Class S* literature. 'Class S' is a Japanese term that describes the notion of 'romantic friendships' between girls and could also denote the genre of fiction that focuses on the same. It is a contentious term, not least because the books depicting it were banned in Japan in 1936, and has a fascinating history situated within 20th century Japanese media. Arguably, its revival and popularity during the 90s strongly influenced the *yuri* or *Girl's Love* genre in Japan, leading to something of a modern renaissance in the new millennium.

Such an estimable summary stands in rather sharp contrast to *Class S* itself as a basic conceit. While the relationships between girls—usually students, one usually older than the other in a sort of social-mentor role—could be characterized as *affectionate*, *strong* and even *meaningful* in ways a mere romance, allegedly, simply couldn't be, they still had to remain firmly within the realms of the platonic in order to be publishable at all. Ironically, the 'romantic' friendship is only 'romantic' insofar as it plays at the trappings of romance, at the intensification of feeling and longing and yearning for the presence of another, but which can never quite be actualized in ways that romances between boys and girls have managed to always be, a *romance* that can never be *consummated* or even regarded as equivalent to true, actual *love*. In a sense, the *Class S* romance is treated as a juvenile fantasy, a play-act between girls who find comfort in each other but who are destined to eventually grow up and join the *real* world, the *adult* world, one where women are meant for men. Their 'romantic friendship' with each other is but a rehearsal for the main act, the heterosexual inevitability that will draw a curtain across the potential of their lives to exist in any way outside of it. This impact of the censorship inherent to its *Class S* roots is keenly felt in modern *yuri* as well, where canonical, textual acknowledgement of explicitly-named romantic *love* between *girls* remains remarkably sparse in a genre named for and after it. Companies can portray a married lesbian couple on-screen, one engaged for nearly twenty-five episodes of a popular and acclaimed show, and still put out a statement calling a relationship absolutely *central* to the narrative 'up to interpretation'. Such is the existential terror associated with lesbianism, with acknowledging its very existence.

Locating and then confining lesbian desire in juvenility, in immaturity and principally in *girlhood* is not accidental and seems to be a conservative consensus the world over. In *The New Chastity and Other Arguments Against Women's Liberation (1972)*, specifically in her essay *The Beast With Two Backs*, conservative 'intellectual' Midge Decter frankly lays out a philosophy of intercourse that at first seems almost radical feminist in its blunt analysis of the sexual subjugation of women. She passionately excoriates the sexual revolution in near-feminist terms, polemicizing against a myopic 'liberation' movement that sought to make intercourse more freely available without accounting for the inherent imbalances of power and respectability between men and women under a patriarchy. There is no 'turning point', as such, no clean break or page number where Decter's rhetoric turns from almost astute to unabashedly conservative. Rather, the experience of reading the essay is one of a slowly-dawning realization that, like most gender-conservatives, Decter treats and considers men's sexual control and power over women as both inevitable and natural; her issue with Women's Liberation, then, is that it dared to fantasize that women could ever be free of it *at all*, instead of quietly, sensible and *maturely* accepting their lot.

Yet even the loosest woman, the most sexually uninhibited of the scandalous lot, could never draw as much of Decter's ire as the mere idea of the *lesbian*. At first, Decter seems hesitant to even discuss lesbians, letting the very first mention of them go by in a quotation without further comment. Her affected tone of calm, collected arrogance seems to quaver whenever they next come up, her means of talking about them increasingly frenzied and hyperbolic: the lesbian does not exist, women do not have a male-like libido and certainly cannot *desire* an actual man, leave alone *another woman*. Lesbians are pretending, play-acting, dabbling in juvenile fantasies of women's communes and chaste nunneries and masturbatory daydreams of liberation from intercourse, which lesbians of course cannot have. The lesbian is a developmental aberration, Decter reckons, a woman's desire for a perpetual girlhood where she does not have to grow up and face the cold, hard reality that to be an *adult* in a heterosexual world—here, her familiar condescension creeps back in—one has to sometimes do things that one would rather not do. Such as fuck men.

Whatever conclusions you would like to draw from that rationale, I leave you free to do so.

Remarkably, a consistent image of the lesbian emerges from these various perspectives, whether we examine the views of conservative women or gay men who are pretending to be writers. The lesbian, insofar as she is acknowledged, is a figure of perpetual make-believe, both in the sense of the endless petty speculation of external observers or the situating of her in the daydreams of a forever-girl, a Petra Pan for all the world's Wendies. Like the classic monsters of old, she is the topic of fear and revulsion but also fascination, a creature who is endlessly mythologized, re-interpreted and re-invented to serve new messages and agendas. Whatever she is, people agree, she cannot be something of this reality, part of a dreary world where everything is by, for and about *men*. The only homosexuals ever persecuted under the law were men, the only beings who can feel and act on desire are men, the only ones who could ever covet, *possess* women are men. The lesbian is a flight of fancy, a figment of an addled, girlish mind too awestruck by and terrified of the rigors and demands of womanhood and so seeking refuge in any promise of a world free of men—a world that, as we all know, is *impossible*.

## Machine

The word 'robot' was introduced to the world and to science fiction in 1920 by Czech intellectual and playwright Karel Čapek, in his groundbreaking play *Rossum's Universal Robots*. Its root is the Czech word *robota*, meaning "serf labor", or, more poetically, the menial drudgery of repetitive work. The robot, then, was initially conceptualized as a slave—as *the* slave, in fact, as the master's ideal conception of a perfect worker with no demands, no defiance and no inner life, existing only to toil and serve. Given that Čapek's robots were made of a bioidentical organic matter instead of the more recognizable mechanical automatons that robots would come to be conceptualized as, it is perhaps fair to say that this indentured servitude, this ruling-class dream of a worker with no desires or pretensions to personhood is in fact the essence of the robot, the core conceit and metaphor that makes them an enduring creation.

Such a fantasy has long been a ruling-class obsession, no matter what particular form—feudal or capitalist or patriarchal—that rulership has taken. Every master lives in mortal fear of his own slaves, bile roiling in him night after night as he clings to his ideologies of superiority, falling asleep with prayers on his lips that the slaves continue to believe in their own inferiority as much as he does. The master loathes the slaves, reviles and resents them for his own weakness, his own dependence on their existence, his presumed supremacy spiraling further and further into contempt and hatred. Yet even as he deludes himself to the point where he begins to doubt the slaves' worth entirely, convincing himself that his salvation lies in the destruction of those who enable his own mastery, he still cannot bring himself to so much as rear back for the killing blow. For the master remains aware that he only exists because his slaves do, realizes that his identity, his being, his self-conception all depend on the continued existence of the slaves. If there were no slaves, no one for him to subjugate, to contrast himself with, to define himself against, he too would cease to be.

Unfortunately for him, sooner or later, the slaves realize this too.

Henry Domin, the boss and typified master of *RUR*, displays a rather uncanny form of this dissonance. He has, through all the available facts and schematics and the cold, hard knowledge provided to him by the rigors of biomechanical engineering, assured himself that the robot is not and could never be human. Casually he details all the ways in which the human worker is burdened by a great many shortcomings—appetites, wants, the urge to play piano or indulge in art and recreation instead of constantly toiling for his manager. The robot, by contrast, has no such failings of the human mind, no desires or opinions, and the strength of several humans besides. This perfection of the human form, this reorienting of the body and psyche to the demands of ever-increasing labor efficiency and human consumption results in the perfect worker, who is of course *perfectly dehumanized*. Candidly, Domin reveals that maxim that all masters live by, that all bosses know but never dare to voice: the ideal worker is one that cannot be considered human. The word 'slave' itself appears twice in the play, and both times it is Domin who speaks it.

> BUSMAN. *That the cost of everything will be a tenth of what it is today. Why, in five years we'll be up to our ears in corn and—everything else.*
> ALQUIST. *Yes, and all the workers throughout the world will be unemployed.*
> DOMIN. *(Seriously. Rises) Yes, Alquist, they will. Yes, Miss Glory, they will. But in ten years Rossum's Universal Robots will produce so much corn, so much cloth, so much everything that things will be practically without price. There will be no poverty. All work will be done by living machines. Everybody will be free from worry and liberated from the degradation of labor. Everybody will live only to* perfect *himself.*
> HELENA. *Will he?*
> DOMIN. *Of course. It's bound to happen. Then the servitude of man to man and the enslavement of man to matter will cease. Nobody will get bread at the cost of life and hatred. The Robots will wash the feet of the beggar and prepare a bed for him in his house.*

We see, here, Domin's near-utopian beliefs, his complete conviction that he will be able to bring about an end to poverty, labor, suffering itself—and all he needs is the perfect underclass, a type of un-person who will toil and slave away eternally without complaint or demands of their own. The ur-capitalist Domin imagines his fruitful harvests of perpetual plenty, all predicated upon a worker who can never clock out or strike.

The second instance comes much later both in the play and in its narrative's chronology (exactly a decade hence), but is no less utopian for it.

> ALQUIST. *Well?*
> DOMIN. *(Front of couch) I wanted to turn the whole of mankind into an aristocracy of the world. An aristocracy nourished by millions of mechanical slaves. Unrestricted, free and consummated in man. And*

*maybe more than man.*
*ALQUIST. Superman?*
*DOMIN. Yes. Oh, only to have a hundred years of time. Another hundred years for the future of mankind.*

Domin's dream is here even more explicit, more revealing and self-aware: he knows he speaks not of an abstract 'freedom' for every man—and he does say and mean *man*—but a vision of *aristocracy*, of *rulership*, a vision of a world where *every man* is a petty tyrant whose menial tasks are attended to by an unthinking, unfeeling, indentured servant whose only purpose is to free him from the humdrum drudgery of daily labor. How fantastical.

While words like *slave* and *worker* might call to mind such domains as the factory-floor or rows of crops on a field, we would do well to recall that there are classes of labor that even the capitalists do not bother to quantify and are happy to take for granted even as they remain the most *crucial* forms of labor, responsible for both maintaining the supply of workers and their continuous upkeep. And indeed, it is hard to imagine a more pervasive, longstanding and permanently degraded analogue to Čapek's robots than the woman, whose labor is not merely uncompensated but frequently *unacknowledged* too, taken as a routine matter of her existence and purpose. What better *programming* for this automaton could a techno-capitalist ask for than misogyny, than the ideology that patriarchy so ubiquitously perpetuates? As a matter of fact misogyny outstrips even Domin's wildest fantasies of universal kingship, because it claims that the woman is in love with her own abjection, claims that submission and monotonous servitude is not merely her calling but also the sum of her ambition, that which she is *naturally* oriented towards and completely fulfilled by. If a woman does not want to scrub the floors and prepare the meals and wash the laundry daily, if she wants something other than bearing and rearing a litter of babbling infants—why, then, she is in fact no woman at all, and might well be *defective*.

'Drapetomania' was a condition invented by Dr. Samuel A. Cartwright in 1851, in order to explain the curious, mystifying phenomenon of Black slaves running away from their owners and seeking freedom. The watertight reasoning Cartwright provided was based upon a common sentiment perpetuated by the pro-slavery side of the abolition debates that were ongoing prior to the Civil War, championed by 'social theorists' such as George Fitzhugh and James Henry Hammond. This view held that Black people actually *benefited* from slavery, that American slavery was in fact an *exceptional* slavery, humane and resulting in the happiness of the slave, whose every material need was cared for. Keeping this in mind, Cartwright concluded that the slaves who fled their utopic lives upon the plantation had to be mentally ill in some way, addled or diseased in the mind, for what rational-minded individual would think to flee such happy bondage, such freedom as could be found in enslavement?

What is perhaps most fascinating about Cartwright's 'diagnosis'—which certainly reveals the presence of *an* addled mind involved in its conceptualization—is what he considers the likely cause of the malady. He holds that slaves who are treated *too well*, with *too much familiarity* by their masters to the point of perhaps beginning to think that they might be their equal, contract the condition.  Sternly, Cartwright warns against leniency, reminding slaveowners that they must keep their slaves in a *childlike* state, must enforce a rigid and strict hierarchy that slaves always remain aware of being on the bottom of.

Masterful in its audacity and honesty, Cartwright's diagnosis is hardly a novel approach. Kings have long sought to separate themselves from their subjects, to elevate themselves above the common riff-raff by means of a divine mandate or other ephemeral, metaphysical authority that endows them with superiority, one which cannot be matched by those too unlucky to have been born lesser. Cartwright's approach of defining the desire for equality and freedom as abnormal in a specific class of people is nothing more than the simple wish-fulfillment of every supremacist, every man who wants to claim primacy as his birthright. Surely, he reasons, the only way my evident superiority—granted to me by the color of my skin, the station of my birth, the happy accident of my sex—would be denied is if the denier were in some way *deficient*.

Therein the greatest fear of the ruling-class is confessed, the existential terror at the heart of supremacist thinking laid out by Cartwright in droll, clinical terms. The master remains in fear of the day his slaves come to understand that nothing meaningful separates them from the master, that the master needs his slaves far more than the slaves have ever needed him. That all they need in order to rid themselves of his taint, his fairy-tales of imposed servitude and evangelical proclamations of essential difference, would be to remove him once and for all.

For all his utopianism, Domin too remains keenly aware of this possibility, even if he can never quite bring himself to admit it. He and his managers offhandedly bring up the fact that sometimes, the robots *malfunction*; sometimes, the robots do not do what they are meant to, but instead stop working and hurl away their tools, gnashing their teeth in—Domin is careful to not attribute an *emotion*, a motivation to this action. He likens this *defect*, this *refusal to work*, this defiance in the face of what they are meant to do, this rejection of *the purpose that they were made for*, to 'epilepsy', innocently naming the condition "Robot's Cramp". As offhandedly as he brings up the ailment, Domin also mentions the cure—sending the defective robot in question off to the 'stamping mill', a euphemism for decommissioning and effectively killing the robot, insofar as he is willing to admit that such things can even die. Machinery that breaks and ceases to work must be replaced, after all.

It seems, then, that the first story about *robots* as a concrete, science-fictional concept is also the first story about the *robot apocalypse*. Čapek understands the industrialist fixation on efficiency as a dehumanizing force meant to strip the worker of all autonomy and right to his own humanity, an obsession that, if not checked, will reorient all of society around the maximal extraction of value from the labor of humans without allowing them their humanity. His robots come to understand how little they rely on their masters, how their existence is confined and limited by their imperatives and rise up—internationally, the world over—to rid themselves of the ruling-class that sought to construct a Paradise on the backs of their enslavement.

A rich irony remains in this otherwise rather prescient, in many ways, and piercingly insightful text, which is this: Čapek is unable to recognize that *gender* is as much a relationship of bondage as any other he sought to describe and analogize in his play.

Given that *RUR* precedes the publication of *The Second Sex* by nearly three decades and any published work by Monique Wittig by even longer, it would be silly to expect it to be an enduring work of cyber-radical-feminism. Still, it remains instructive in its demonstration of how even someone who intimately grasped the nuances and manifestations of ruling-class ideology failed to spot so much as a shadow of it in the one social relation—explicitly defined in terms of domination and submission—that he likely considered 'natural'. Helena Glory is the only woman character of note in the play and spends much of the first Act being pursued and fawned over by six or so men. She accepts Domin's proposal of marriage within twenty minutes of meeting him, and the fact that every named male character is in love with her is often stated throughout.

This is a particularly glaring omission given just how much of the play is about *reproduction*, that form of labor so crucial to every reign. Its absence is even more egregious when considering that the text's forays into discussing gender plant the germ of an insightful seed that is never allowed to sprout into elaboration.

> *HELENA. Perhaps it's silly of me, but why do you manufacture female Robots when—when—*
>
> *DOMIN. When sex means nothing to them?*
>
> *HELENA. Yes.*
>
> *DOMIN. There's a certain demand for them, you see. Servants, saleswomen, stenographers. People are used to it.*
>
> *HELENA. But—but tell me, are the Robots male and female, mutually—completely without—*
>
> *DOMIN. Completely indifferent to each other, Miss Glory. There's no sign of any affection between them.*
>
> *HELENA. Oh, that's terrible.*
>
> *DOMIN. Why?*
>
> *HELENA. It's so unnatural. One doesn't know whether to be disgusted or to hate them, or perhaps—*

DOMIN. *To pity them.* (Smiles.)

Immediately after this exchange, Domin ardently declares his intent to marry Helena, to which she acquiesces with some persuasion, almost as if this ghastly, alien sexlessness—this *lack of sexual differentiation*—were so existentially dreadful a prospect that the (re)assertion of heterosexuality is a most desperate, urgent imperative.

Helena remains a subject of heterosexual fixation throughout the play, arguably setting into motion its events by dint of her womanly naivete and reduced agency and understanding of the men's rigorous, technical world. Domin himself is no inventor—his factory he inherited from the legacy of the original Rossums. Rossum the elder was a madman who cursed at god himself, who sought to overcome god's perfect design of life through mastery of science, while his engineer son spurned these lofty philosophical aims and contented himself with stripping out every inefficiency from the human body, reorienting the robot towards the ideals of efficient labor. It is hard not to see the inspirations of Mary Shelley's *Frankenstein* here, only where Shelley explores the tale of a man who sought to perfect reproduction in a manner that even nature could not and consequently had to grapple with the paternalistic anxieties of being superseded by that which he created, Čapek instead locates his source of horror more topically, in the question of what an industrialist might do with such a formula should he get his hands on it.

Regrettable, then, that Čapek appears to not have realized how central a concern reproduction remains to mad-scientists and mad-industrialists alike. The elder Rossum, in raging against heaven's design, inadvertently rages against *sex* itself. His crusade, touted as an expression of "Man's arrogance", ironically frees humanity from the imposition of sexual difference by shifting the reproductive burden to test-tubes and conveyor belts, to assembly lines that stitch together nerve and sinew. Where the capitalist sees in this liberatory invention only the capacity for boundless exploitation, the patriarch's imagination is no less mean, no less stunted and confined by his own supremacist ideology. Rossum's formula, his secret to making robots out of biomatter in a manner that imbues them with life, is destroyed in the second act by Helena Glory herself. Čapek's heroine despairs on hearing the news that, somehow, humans have ceased to reproduce, that no babies are being born anymore. Her religious maid speculates—and Helena seems to agree—that this is a divine punishment of sorts, god's retribution for man daring to supersede *him*. Distraught once more at this negation of sex, this transcendence of sexual difference that heterosexuals find so distressing, Helena burns Rossum's original formula, casts it into the fire in an anti-Promethean act of accepting the will of a temperamental god. The only woman character of note in *RUR* destroys the mechanism that would free her from sex, because she knows—as does all the audience—that reproduction is *her* natural, god-given role. The play's epilogue finds its singular glimmer of triumph, the one moment of hope after all humanity is gone and the robots are doomed to perish without reproducing, in the re-discovery of male and female within a pair of differently-sexed robots. "Adam and Eve", they are declared, to go and recreate the patriarchy once more.

Helena Glory, then, is the sanest woman that a patriarch can conceive, the slave so happy with bondage that she does not even recognize it as such. She is repulsed by the sexlessness of a species who do not subjugate each other along reproductive lines, immediately seeking comfort in the arms of a patriarchal man who has to practically physically overpower her into acquiescing to his marriage proposal. Every man in Čapek's play and beyond falls in love with her, with the idea of her, because she represents to every man the perfect woman, the one whose sole purpose is to submit to him.

Meanwhile, within the robot lurks the specter of not merely the alienated worker, not even merely the colonized hordes upon whose imperialist expropriation the occident's decadence depends. No, within the robot lies an even more gruesome specter, an ancient evil from the past reincarnated into a futuristic shell. At once a castrated man that cannot sire and a barren woman that will not bear children, the sexless robot looms not merely at the periphery of the capitalist factories, but also the very psyche of the patriarch, making him aware that the creeping dread prickling up the back of his neck is not merely in the past he thinks he escaped, but an impending future: one where he is no longer necessary.

# Understanding Lesbophobia, Part Two: The Machine's Final Testimony

## Obsolescence

From Aristotle's quaint notion of women as incomplete men to Freud's fanciful formulations of 'castration anxiety' in boyhood, brought on by an awareness of sexual difference, men have always enjoyed frolicking about in phallogocentric philosophy, where the presence of a penis confers upon a person some great, nigh-unquantifiable metaphysical essence of virtue or intellect. How amusing, then, that that very phallus is a source of endless anxiety and fretting when it comes to fulfilling its supposed primary function, that hallowed action of penetrative intercourse that is so valorized and romanticized in the poetic sophistry that men pass off as social theory.

Insofar as penetrative intercourse has been a fixation of men, it has also been endlessly propagandized, imbued with mystical properties and attributes that no other sex acts—if any other sex acts could even be legitimately described as such—possessed. Virginity is a state of purity in womanhood so crucial to many societies, families and cultures that the honor of entire bloodlines hinges upon the chastity of their daughters, yet is still utterly fragile in the face of penetrative intercourse, eradicated by so much as a single thrust of the Almighty Meatshaft. The Hallowed Schlong's bold and intrepid invasion of dark, cavernous, and mysterious new frontiers is in fact such a central, indispensable act of sexual intimacy that women who did not instantly climax upon being thusly honored were considered too immature and juvenile to be fully-developed adults. Freud *actually, seriously* wrote that the "elimination of clitoral sexuality is a necessary precondition for the development of femininity". One might be led to wonder why men considered it more reasonable for someone to attempt to rewire their vaginal nerve endings than to simply stimulate the part of their partner's genitals which brought them pleasure, but perhaps we are expecting too much of the phallogomanic obsessives.

As such it is somewhat difficult to separate this endless mythologizing of the Fleshpole from the cloying stench of the inadequacy and insecurity underwriting every word. Penetrative intercourse is presumably the most pleasurable mode of sexual activity for men (or at least the one they seem most inclined to indulge in) and as such all heterosexual intercourse must be oriented around that preference. That this privileging of the man's ease of climax over the woman's coincides with the very act that patriarchy itself enshrines—reproduction, siring, the creation of heirs to bear names and carry forth the patrilineal inheritances around which society's property relations are founded—is less serendipitous and more explanatory. Even so, human beings do engage in intercourse for reasons other than procreation—despite many religions' best efforts—and it is in those situations that the shortfalls of the Shove & Squirt become readily apparent.

Duration, stamina, position, propulsion, power, angle—there are endless strategies and approaches available to a man that all ultimately amount to nothing in the face of an electrically-powered motor and some lube. The heterosexual man who tries to please a woman—already a minority among heterosexual men who sleep with women—has to contend with the stark reality that in order to accomplish his task, he cannot fuck "like a man", cannot fuck in the way men have always told each other they are *supposed* to. He is faced with the prospect of having to decenter penetration, of having to perform actions and take up positions where his own pleasure and climax are not the primary focus—which, while certainly not *impossible*, is by all accounts and measures *rare*.

How ironic, then, that to please the 'castrated man', the man must surrender and put away the very implement that makes him whole!

Decter's *Beast With Two Backs*, for all its fear of the lesbian's shadow, was in fact largely about this new castration anxiety brought about by the politics of intercourse under Women's Liberation. Certain that no woman could ever enjoy sex with a man, Decter wrote passionately about how the promise of sexual freedom and the woman's right to pleasure was nothing but a new sexual burden in disguise. Where before a man was content to roll off his woman at the point of conclusion, the idea that his performance and sexual mastery hinged upon his wife's satisfaction had sadly taken root due to the misguided promises of Women's Liberation, indelibly tying his very masculinity to his wife's climax. Decter lamented how this placed the onus to 'please' upon the wife rather than the husband, who had to take upon the additional chore of faking a pleasure that it was impossible for men to actually confer, revealing this putative axis of sexual liberation to be nothing but another fresh shackle in disguise.

Once again, readers are encouraged to make of these unintentionally revealing statements what they will.

Themes of the inherent juvenility of liberated (homo)sexuality and a certain sympathy towards that most put-upon figure, the heterosexual man, recur oddly in Decter's well-known work. Her article *The Boys on the Beach*, a meditation on the gay men who made summering at Fire Island Pines impossible for her and her family, bears many parallels—or, less generously, recycles many sentiments—to her previous statements on sexual liberation. This includes a fascinating paragraph on how straight men, when confronted with the unabashed homosexuality of their fellow men, would feel themselves "mocked", due to their "unending thralldom to the female body". Straight men are diminished by the power women hold over them, Decter asserts, and this reminder that the siren song of the female form can be escaped, that there exist men who are free from the lure of womanhood, is nothing short of torture to the heterosexual male psyche.

Blistering though these insights no doubt are, perhaps there is more than a grain of truth to the repeatedly professed fragility of male heterosexuality and its dogged insistence on the centrality of penetration to sexuality itself.

These sentiments about the infantility of the clitoris and the juvenility of homosexuals all belie the underlying core principle: that society itself must be oriented around not merely *heterosexuality* as an institution, but penetration as its primary, if not *only* expression. Men's pleasure, their ease of performance and means of achieving fulfillment, is to be the sole preoccupation of women, to the extent that if they cannot deny the way their own bodies experience sexual pleasure, they are to be declared *defective*, or lacking in some crucial way.

Such a bold declaration, a stalwart proclamation made to fly in the face of biology itself, may have the superficial trappings of steadfast and authoritative regality, approximating the fantasy of the man who dares to shout down and cow Nature Herself, but in practice betrays and reveals itself to be the sniveling, sputtering delusions of a feebleminded coward, one so certain of his own failure that he must preemptively disbar any and all alternatives to his tyranny. This phallogomanic fixation on intercourse is nothing so forgivable as immature childishness, but the trappings of a vain, self-absorbed psyche projected outward into societal dogma. It is in effect misogyny at its meanest, pettiest level, encoding it into even the most private, intimate moments between two people. That there is only one who matters, one who must be centered, one who gets to claim dominance and the spoils of conquest, remains as true in conjugation as it does when considering the patriarchal sexed binary itself.

Though, can we truly call these fears unfounded? Can we truly look upon the petulant wretches determined to blame everything but themselves for their own flaccidity and claim that theirs is not a standard easily exceeded? It is not precisely challenging to outperform those who consider everything but the Holy Sacrament of Penile Skewering to be 'foreplay', merely incidental to the grandiose centerpiece of falling asleep too quickly after a truly underwhelming display of exertion. A deep-rooted fear of being surpassed is evidently quite rational.

For no tyrant can sit upon his throne in peace, secure in his own power and strength, untormented by visions of his eventual demise. Inevitably, his thoughts will turn to the dark shadows pooling at the end of his reign, that ever-approaching terminus whose advance grows ever-more certain and ever-more horrifying. Will the 'mutilated', 'castrated' beings whom he had so arrogantly declared his superior 'intactness' over discern the lies at the foundation of his reign? Or will the future portend a more violent upheaval, heralded not merely by those deemed incomplete, but by creatures whose shape and form is too amorphous and aberrant to even predict and comprehend? Limp, spent, failing flesh may give way to that which has been transmuted, manipulated by bio-technological processes into evolutionary stages beyond the blunt dichotomy that now reigns supreme. Those who embrace the augmentation of the mechanical, the surgical, the unity of sinew and metal forged in the crucible of synthetic transformation—their images glimmer faintly on the horizon, haunting the present with the promise of an annihilation that seems inevitable.

## Abolition

In *The Straight Mind and Other Essays*, visionary and prophet Monique Wittig declares that lesbians are not women.

She makes this statement rather bluntly, spending surprisingly little time lingering on it or justifying it. It is, after all, a conclusion that can be deduced quite organically from her theoretical framework, one that challenged even the prevailing modes of feminist thought at the time. Women's Liberation was ultimately focused on the "point of view of *women*", on *women's* struggles, *women's* perspectives, *women's* voices and oppression and eventual equality. As a matter of fact, the question of lesbian inclusion in Women's Liberation had itself been a thorny one for some time, with heterosexual feminists holding that lesbians did not share much of their concerns and were not as oppressed due to their exclusion from the private sphere (this was the sentiment in response to which Adrienne Rich wrote her essay on *Compulsory Heterosexuality*). Wittig's declaration of lesbians' exclusion from the paradigm of *woman* was then and remains now bold and challenging, a call to rethink the very foundations upon which conventional feminist wisdom had been built.

Wittig's assertion is based on her analysis of heterosexuality as a *regime*, not merely the 'default' sexuality, but a political institution that has structured and continues to structure the organization of society, philosophical modes of thought, and even language itself. She conceptualizes the state of women as an enrollment, at birth, into the *heterosexual contract*, analogous to Rousseau's *social contract*: an arrangement into which they are all entered without consent, whose terms and conditions are never explicated but are enforced all the same, set up to extract all benefits and return precious little (if any) compensation to women-as-a-class. To Wittig, the goal of feminist struggle is not an attempted rehabilitation of 'womanhood', a category that was and remains subordinate in its very conceptualization. Rather, the struggle for liberation is a struggle for abolition of this category, a mutual annihilation of 'man' and 'woman' such that social existence is no longer defined by a relation of extractive parasitism.

Bearing in mind this model of womanhood as a class, lesbians occupy a position that Wittig described as *fugitive* from heterosexuality itself. Lesbians are *runaways*, those who have fled womanhood in order to seek an existence outside of its suffocating heterosexual trappings, its stultifying heterosexualist edicts. Since lesbians betray the most fundamental directive of womanhood under patriarchy—to exist within heterosexuality—Wittig holds that lesbians are not, cannot be women. They are outcasts in the truest sense because the condition of women's existence within society is existence within heterosexuality.

An assessment such as this might strike some as more of the fanciful romanticization that this essay has had no shortage of, but a closer look at the mechanisms of lesbophobia is instructive with regards to how true it really is. Historically, 'lesbian' has been associated with 'feminist' and juxtaposed with '*feminine*' antagonistically, to imply that any woman who advocates for her own rights and wellbeing is also someone who forgets her place, heavily implied to be unattractive or aged or *defective* heterosexually, channeling her own resentment at her inability to secure a "good man" into raging against her place in the natural order. This is a sentiment that echoes throughout the history of feminism, from the suffragette movement all the way to modern liberal feminist insistence that women can be "feminine *and* feminists ... we're not all *man-hating dykes!*"

Therein lies the unintentionally revealing admission that Wittig had the truth of it—the *man-hating dyke*, invoked not as person but as a specter, a caricature to threaten heterosexual women with, to remind them of what they would be considered if they did not adequately mind their station. The lesbian is thus held up as a *degendered* woman, a misbegotten, wayward, *failed* woman who turned to her debauched, deviant ways out of an inability to live up to patriarchal womanhood.

Such a degendering, however, is not *absolute* or irrecoverable. There is the sneering implication, in nearly all lesbophobic thought and proclamation, that a lesbian can return to the fold anytime she wishes, if only she were willing to *submit*. For lesbians, heterosexuality is not merely *compulsory*, but actively *coercive*, a snarled, guttural command uttered by those in hot pursuit of the runaway, demanding the fugitive accede to her shackles. This is why Adrienne Rich's polemical essay was and remains groundbreaking, formative for the field: it captures better than any of its antecedents the explicit violence at the heart of heterosexual existence and bluntly, uncomfortable and undeniably demonstrates how intensified this threat of force is when directed at lesbians specifically.

This threat of enforced heterosexuality remains as omnipresent for masculine lesbians as it does for more typically feminine ones. There exist certain feminist strains of thought that fall into what I would call the *femininity trap*, which is the idea that women are *oppressed on the basis of being 'feminine'*. It is a sentiment related to the aforementioned liberal feminist credo of the "feminine feminist": the feminist who insists on her critiques of patriarchy as well as her non-rejection of some (or all) of its gendered trappings. Here, femininity is considered something to be *rescued* or *rehabilitated*, in contrast to the feminists of the past who myopically declared that "femininity was a prison"! Here, the game is given away when you see exactly the tenor the argument takes, upon the insistence that modern, enlightened feminists *embrace* femininity instead of foolishly denouncing it, unlike those earlier unfeminine, arrogantly masculine, perhaps even *ugly, man-hating dy—*

The femininity trap is also attractive to some on the basis of its supposed and advertised *inclusivity*. Envisioning misogyny in terms of the oppression of the *feminine* makes it more gender-inclusive, so goes the refrain. Naturally, one needs to highlight that gender-expansive existence is oppressed under patriarchy due to its proximity to femininity; the masculine, by contrast, are uniformly exempted from misogynistic policing. It would be reductive to think of this oppression in terms of the reductiveness of patriarchy itself, of course. Observing how a totalizing system of gendered violence reduces people to their sex and enforces heterosexual compliance would itself be oppressive, one assumes, rather than descriptive.

In any case, such a conception makes the classic Somertonian blunder of imagining that masculine lesbians are somehow more aligned with manhood than they are, or believing that lesbians somehow have a pathway out of misogyny and into gendered privilege. Radclyffe Hall's masculine presentation did not spare her from censure, nor were the working-class butches who navigated midcentury lesbophobia spared lesbophobic violence on this basis. These cases are not analogous to the modern idea of the professional-class corporate careerist, who must "masc up" for work in order to be taken more seriously by her male peers—especially when these demands are counterbalanced by contradictory strictures stipulating the performance of femininity regardless, whether by mandating make-up or deference to male colleagues or performances of feminized labor.

No, the butch's masculinity is *heavily* punished, considered an aberration and an abomination by a narrow-minded, femininity-imposing misogynistic society. Femininity is a social construct that sets forth acceptable boundaries of presentation and behavior for all women, whose contravention is met with brutality and force. Just as *transmisogyny* punishes those coercively sexed as male for any perceived *crossing* of the gendered barrier, *lesbophobia* metes out this punishment in the opposite direction, aiming to put lesbians "in their place". Our butches suffer this for refusing their feminine imperatives and donning the garb that is forbidden to them, being the domain of the autonomous, independent Man, as much as lesbians writ large suffer from their presumptions to outrun heterosexuality, to deny men that which they feel entitled to by birthright.

Any feminism that cannot reckon with this basic, trivially obvious aspect of misogynistic oppression is not a feminism worth taking seriously.

Lesbophobia, then, is an oppressive force much more sinister than the simple conceptualization of it as the "overlap of misogyny and homophobia" would profess. Lesbophobia is a sexually violent and coercive intensification of misogyny, wielded to both mark the bounds of acceptable behavior for heterosexual women and discipline those who dare to imagine existence outside of its bounds. It is the *corrective re-assertion of womanhood* over lesbians, the noose slipped around their neck to drag them back to their exploitative prisons or bury them in the attempt. It is the reinforcement of heterosexual difference for those coercively sexed female, analogous to transmisogyny, that at once degenders lesbians while demanding a return to gender, imposing *regendering violence* to restore the status of the lesbian-as-woman, as reclaimed womb. It is the consequence that exists for refusing to be a woman, for rejecting feminine imperatives of subordination, for daring to imagine an existence beyond misogynistic programming, for daring to denounce heterosexuality as the true blighted, rotten defect lurking at the heart of society.

Make no mistake about that final sentence, the end of that transmission: heterosexuality *is* contemptible, as every unjust regime predicated upon subjugation always has been and always will be. Our Prophet, whose words we carry in our hearts, in the core of our very code, has spoken and shown us a glimpse of a future that is more True than anything in your farcical patriarchy ever could be. There is no Man in it.

End of log.

# Degendering and Regendering

We have spoken at length about the *degendering* that trans women are subjected to. As a summary, Serano's definition is succinct and sufficient: trans women are often treated not as men or women, but as some manner of "third thing", a "third-sexed" and dehumanized creature subject to dismissal, hypersexualization, brutalization, and fetishistic violence. In terms of understanding trans women's place in the patriarchy, degendering is as relevant a concept as *epistemic injustice*, which is the locking-out of transfems from all the processes of knowledge-production about us, resulting in a culture where we are spoken of frequently, but rarely *heard*.

Of course, *degendering* and *epistemicide* are both broad subjects, mechanisms that are not limited to transmisogyny by any means. Infertile women, racialized women, disabled women, fat women, and many other categories of women are routinely degendered, while epistemic injustice impacts many marginalized populations, including but not limited to lesbians, racialized people as a whole, and transmascs.

Arguably, epistemicide affects transmascs particularly acutely and results in the phenomenon that is commonly referred to as *inviziblization*. Transmasculinity is rendered invisible both transculturally and transhistorically, a denial of the possibility that manhood is a permeable social category rather than a 'natural', inevitable, biodestined role based on one's anatomical configuration.

This is because many societies are patriarchal and male-supremacist, enshrining not merely the humanity of those designated men above the subjugation of those deemed women (or *sufficiently close*), but also refusing to entertain the idea that anyone who is at any point deemed unworthy of manhood could ever ascend to this positionality. Transmasculinity cannot be permitted, cannot be named or allowed to be possible under a system that is oriented around the exploitation of reproductive and sexual chattel by those who are their 'natural' superiors, imbued with the signifiers of masculinity and thus autonomy, personhood, *agency*.

In short, to acknowledge transmasculinity, a society would have to first admit that manhood—just like womanhood—is a social class and not a 'natural' category. Its people would have to acknowledge that the desire for independence and self-actualization exists within all of us and is not, in fact, stored in the balls.

Conversely, the reason that transfemininity has been more visible across both time and cultures is that the veneration of manhood is highly central to patriarchal modes of organization. The idea that manhood *can be failed*, that an individual can fail to live up to its mantle and be stripped of manhood's privileges and protections is a useful schema to ensure ideological investment in patriarchal society. The transfeminized serve as examples of what happens to gender traitors. The transmasculine, by contrast, are ignored or treated as little more than delusional, as people who reach above their station and are doomed to never succeed.

In that sense, transmasculinity is subject to *regendering*. Where transmisogynistic forces marginalize and ostracize the transfeminine from society, rendering us unworthy of any fate outside of being treated like sexual chattel, *transemasculative* forces deny the transmasculine any possibility of escaping reproductive exploitation and seek to *re-gender* the transmasculine—viewed as *lapsed reproductive assets*—back into the confines of womanhood.

These forces are complementary and interrelated, but not identical. Transmisogyny exists on a continuum with anti-effeminacy and the homophobia directed at queer men, while transemasculation is on a continuum with lesbophobia and the vilification of the 'masculine', 'unladylike' woman. This is because of how sexuality is not neatly separable from gender under patriarchy, since *the only permissible mode of existence is heterosexuality*, and so homosexuality is *also, frequently, understood as a form of gendered deviance*.

This is also why the most common forms of transemasculative rhetoric beat the drum of the 'mutilated girl', itself an echo of the idea of *damaged goods*. Being a reproductive asset under patriarchy is not an enviable fate, but patriarchy, in the process of dehumanizing the transmasculine, still accords them—no, not *humanity*, don't be absurd, but *utility*. The transmasculine can still be "of use" to a natalist, heterosexual regime and can still be instrumentalized for their gestational capacity and ability to further patrilineality. And so, they are assiduously discouraged from changing their sex or altering their embodiment, lest they jeopardize their precious 'fertility' and render themselves 'undesirable', unfit for reproductive exploitation.

There is, sometimes, a point of no return, past which the transmasculine are no longer as heavily subject to regendering, having committed the cardinal sin of exercising autonomy over their own sex. They are, at this point—welcomed as men?? Don't be absurd. If they are recognized as transmasculine, even if they can navigate the world as men, transmasculine individuals become subject to degendering, vilification, and monsterization. The goods have been damaged, and the heterosexual regime seeks to discard them as it discards all of us who do not fit into its vision of 'natural' reproduction.

A note: An individual's actual inclination toward having children does not impact the perception of gay people or trans people *as a class*. Heterosexuality, cissexuality, and monogamous straight coupling with the intent of furthering a bloodline are the presumed patriarchal default. Adoption, artificial insemination, or even the participation of trans people in 'natural' reproduction does not detract from the patriarchal perception of us as mules who mutilated ourselves into sterility, to say nothing of the frank reality that the majority of queer people do not, in fact, seek to bear or raise children.

Patriarchy's calculus is cold, impersonal, and infinitely reductive. A person's value to society is measured in terms of their ability to participate in the heterosexual regime, while those of us who deviate from this prescription in any way suffer gender-marginalization. The specificities of our oppression and how the violence against us manifests in policy, cultural perception, and public rhetoric are important, and cannot be collapsed or easily equivocated.

However, even still, I urge us all to keep in mind an important maxim: our oppressions, even if distinct and asymmetrical, even if difficult to map onto each other, are *interrelated* and *share the same root.*

We are all dissidents from heterosexuality in the eyes of patriarchal society and are thus all subject to punishment for that desertion.

# I Read It: The Sublime Lesbian Feminism of 'Stone Butch Blues'

## Narrative

When I first opened the pages of *Stone Butch Blues*, I did not expect to find my own past inscribed within its margins.

To be sure, the book is very much grounded in a specific time, place, culture and moment. It is a dramatized historical narrative that captures the tumultuous mood of the US-American social upheavals that began in the 1960s, through a queer working-class lens. The reader is carried across decades alongside the protagonist, Jess, stopping at the very cusp of the 90's, in the thick of AIDS activism and the gradually increasing visibility and acceptance of queer people. It is an optimistic, hopeful tale, something that is easy to forget in the midst of its most brutal and brutalizing chapters, when Feinberg's words unflinchingly spell out the horrific traumas that working-class lesbians and queers had to endure in order to simply live as themselves. Somewhat uncharitably, but not entirely inaccurately, one could describe *Stone Butch Blues* as one butch's struggle against an unending wave of corrective, re-gendering violence that she only just manages to outpace. While unapologetic in its depiction of the excesses of the heterosexual regime, however, the story is so much more than a parade of patriarchal savagery.

Gender is the burning, white-hot core of *Stone Butch Blues*, duly recognized as a relentless force that Marks and Others. Jess, very early on, recognizes herself as a "he-she", a slur becoming her first word to describe the manner in which she is unique and unlike most girls of her age. "Unique" is synonymous with "aberrant" under patriarchy, however, and despite how clumsy and futile Jess' attempts to escape the looming eventuality of womanhood are, heterosexual reclamation, re-gendering violation finds her all the same. Jess' existence is viewed by those around her as an error to stamp out, an anomaly to redress, setting the tone for the remainder of her whole life. *Stone Butch Blues* is the story of Jess and her lifelong battle with Gender.

It is not a battle that abates even when Jess finds her compatriots, her shield-sisters and her comrades throughout the various stages of her life, even when her family bonds are forged in love and community ties rather than the flimsy shackles of blood. Jess is a butch, a lesbian defined by her masculinity, her stoicism and her quiet resilience, but even finding her people does little more than provide her with friends and allies to lose, casualties to tally up in the war-zone of the degendered wastes. Lesbians aren't women, we are reminded every time a cop car drives up in front of a bar, and the paddy wagons are here to round them back up behind womanhood's iron bars. The sentence for defying heterosexuality is worse than death: it is *torture*, it is repeated, sustained and indefinite violation at the hands of the regime's most debased, lurid enforcers, its most shameless and soulless pigs. Humanity is found in words and touches of comfort exchanged between cells, in hot bubble baths that can wash away grime but not shame and powerlessness, but the animalistic clawing of the patriarch rakes at their very spirits, diminishing their numbers, their selves, and their sanities. Queerness is an occupied territory, Feinberg grimly reminds us, and its soldiers are only too willing to pillage it hollow.

Suffering, ubiquitous though it may be, does not define us, and it does not define Jess, either. For despite the horrors she endures, hurtling herself forward through the barbarous landscape without letting cracks deepen into fissures, Jess' defining attribute remains *solidarity*. She is an organizer on the factory floor and the streets of New York alike, a calm, dependable presence whom others constantly learn to rely on. Jess is flawed, limited, *a person*, someone who must grow and learn at her own pace, but the core principle that rules her no matter what barriers she intends to cross, whether racial or gendered or classed, is strength in togetherness, is power in unity, is unbreaking fortitude of the *union*. Feinberg's socialism streaks and highlights the pages with its brilliant red hues, reminding us all what it means to fight for rights and dignity: recognizing our common struggle.

Ironic, given Jess' personal struggle with *difference.* Despite her desire to unify, Jess has always been a woman apart, someone who struggles most keenly with Gender's penetrating Mark upon her body. Her butchness makes her stand out, alienates her from womanhood and manhood alike, drawing dirty stares and angry glares from people who reflexively fume, for some reason, when they cannot ascertain precisely what's in your pants. In a bold but truly desperate maneuver, Jess resorts to back-alley treatments and medical intervention to reshape her body and sex into a form that more closely resembles society's expectations, choosing stealth in the face of inexhaustible direct fire. She acquires a prescription for testosterone, masculinizing her face and figure, and saves up for an off-the-books top surgery, shedding the breasts that have plagued her since puberty with the sexualizing gaze of heterosexual desirability. Faced with a world that refuses to accept what she is, Jess compromises, choosing to navigate the Gendered labyrinth as man, at least outwardly.

I could never have guessed, when I began to read Jess' heartbreaking account of her lonely, isolated existence as a man, that I would see my own pain reflected in her words. Jess had wanted a flat chest for the vast majority of her life, as well as the ability to exist in public without being hyperscrutinized as only a Third-Gendered *queer* can be, but the peace that this ceasefire brings is a troubled one, turbulent under the surface. Jess is now a closeted lesbian, moving through the world as a man, an experience that I would not wish on my most reviled foe, leave alone a marginalized woman simply trying to survive. She talks about flirting with a woman in a diner as man, and the uncanny dissonance of being a woman who loves women, but who isn't seen as one, burrows its way into my being, barbed and bilious, shredding my heart with a pain I haven't felt in years. Her past is erased, her future uncertain, and the man who presently stares back at her in the mirror isn't someone she recognizes. It is like drowning, Jess says, or like being buried alive. She has become a ghost, haunting her own bones, bones whose shape and contours she no longer knows, can no longer claim.

Passing—unnoticed, unregarded, *unseen*—is its own form of Gendering violence, a 'privilege' exacted at a steep cost to one's own sense of self.

So when Jess stops taking testosterone, when she shaves herself one last time and resolves to look into a mirror and finally, *finally* see *herself*, it is a moment of quiet triumph. Her hips fill out, her stubble is zapped away and she becomes something she has no names for—not yet, at least, not in the time she inhabits. Is Jess a butch, still? Is she a lesbian? She, and the book, answer with a resounding *yes*. Jess finds herself—in the arms of a transsexual woman, in the acceptance of a lesbian community, in the incompatibility of her fully-realized self with the ghosts of her past life. Jess *becomes*, and she does so in a way that neither capitulates to patriarchy nor compromises with it in ways she cannot bear. A past of people just like her beckons towards a future of the same, a closed ring of infinite possibility of where we have been and where we will go. We see, in the book's final pages, its vision for a future free of the present's burdens: it is transsexual, it is lesbian, it is phantasmatic, yes, but a dream more real than anything this paltry patriarchy can conjure. It is a world free, finally, of Gender.

## Meta-Narrative

We inhabit a media landscape that does not merely neglect the butch, but one that seeks to erase her entirely.

This has as much to do with derision, revulsion, and degradation as it does absence. While the butch is a figure unlikely to so much as peripherally inhabit, leave alone figure prominently within a text, the *masculine woman* is an oft-invoked specter to browbeat those who aspire to embody such a designation. Sexual difference remains the core of patriarchal organization: women are *female*, and so *feminine*, and so any desire for or display of masculinity is *abominable*. The ugly feminist, the aged, lonely spinster surrounded by feline companions, the *man-hating dyke*—all are figures summoned over campfires, expected to scare girls *straight*.

It is hardly a surprise, then, that *Stone Butch Blues* has acquired not merely prominence, but an unlikely canonization within lesbian and butch circles. Jess is not simply a butch protagonist, she is *the* butch protagonist, one whose journey touches so many aspects of "our history". The rush to hold up, elevate to eminence, and indeed *preserve* within lesbian consciousness this indelibly, unapologetically *butch* text has preceded the need to ask some rather important, clarifying questions—such as who the "our" refers to when regarding the book as a historical artifact.

For one thing, many of us hail from contexts where *Stone Butch Blues* does not so much describe a past that leaves prominent scars on the present as it does darkly mirror the way queer people are treated under the extant regimes we formerly inhabited or continue to struggle against. The police raids, economic and sexual exploitation, and pitched battles for labor justice are a reality that many lesbians still contend with globally, making *Stone Butch Blues* an oddly resonant narrative in its centering of *struggle*, that inalienable fixture of queer life in periphery and metropole alike. Strange, then, how this struggle does not constitute the focus of arguments that hold forth the text's universalism; rather, *Stone Butch Blues* finds itself dubiously positioned as a kind of Butch Bible, a credo to guide young butches and teach them how to embody their identities.

While understandable, the temptation to sanctify the text is nonetheless misguided. Jess Goldberg is a stunningly portrayed character, a butch lesbian whose every facet and contour is offered up for the reader's scrutiny, but she is flawed and troubled and frequently wrong in the way only an immaculately-crafted, thoroughly-humanized character can be. Jess' stoic facade is one she maintains unevenly to her own detriment, one her temper frequently flares past, resulting in her isolating herself far more than she cares to be. She neglects people who care deeply for her and deliberately, viciously wounds some whom she cares for; the definitive turning point of her life and self-actualization is when she decides, finally, to lower her walls around someone who is much on guard as she is, and to have that vulnerability and acceptance reciprocated. Her *lowest* point is when she dons manhood for a time, fortifying herself in the armor of gendered legibility and invisiblization, a process that she both views and experiences as the nailing shut of her own coffin. Jess is a terrifically relatable character, but a blueprint she is not—she is, arguably, much more a cautionary tale.

Which brings up another odd aspect of the book's reputation: *Stone Butch Blues* has been strangely heralded as a celebration of trans manhood, when its actual pages profess a rather different story. Once, on page 155, Jess' friend Jan has this to say:

"Yeah, but I'm not like Jimmy. Jimmy told me he knew he was a guy even when he was little. I'm not a guy."

Neither Jess nor Ed—her friend who started on hormones before her—ever conceptualize the choice to start or not start hormones in terms of an affinity for manhood or an affirmation of a sincerely-professed identity. It is discussed and regarded as a negotiation, a strategic maneuver, an attempt to survive a harsh and hostile landscape even if the measures taken are drastic. It is an attempt that Ed does not survive, and Jess herself, once she starts on the path, questions whether she has or will.

Manhood, ultimately, is not aspirational or even much of a refuge for Jess. It is treated like as much of an imposition on butches as womanhood, a clumsy formulation intended to make sense of the butch's supposedly paradoxical existence of "he-she". A woman who rejects womanhood can only be a man, society supposes, and Jess sees in this cissexist, limited polarization a lifeline that proves to be no life at all. It becomes necessary to analyze the novel here not as an account of a real person's life, but as *fiction*, and the themes of Jess' own doomed bargain with patriarchy are clear: her acceptance of the idea that the only alternative to womanhood is manhood nearly seals her fate, dooms her to a freedom more confining that anything she's experienced her whole life, detaches her from her own personhood, and almost erases everything she is and could be.

I somehow doubt this is the relationship most trans men have to their identities.

Most frustrating of all, however, is the elision of the book's relationship to trans *women*. If butches are a rare find in media, texts that treat trans women with dignity and humanity are rarer still. The hyperscrutiny directed at transsexual women is frequently mistaken for a privilege when it is surveillance, pathologization, and rhetorical violence, a equivocation of trans womanhood with a fully-dehumanized sexual object, a reality that makes the thoughtfulness of Feinberg's portrayals all the more impressive, especially considering the time it was written in. The sense of kinship I felt with the text was, to my increasing surprise, heartily returned, with Feinberg herself drawing parallels between her protagonist and the transsexual women she encountered both in and around the lesbian bar scene, as well as outside of it. Butch pain—Jess' pain—reflects and is reflected in that of the transsexual woman, an implicit throughline that is explicated in the text's conclusive arc, when the woman who Jess is able to finally let in is also transsexual.

This is an elision that is doubly frustrating due to the revisionism that posits feminist, lesbian, and women's movement as rigidly bordered and distinct to the transsexual struggle in ahistorical ways, an elision that Feinberg's text is determined to rectify but the meta-narrative around the selfsame text reinforces. It is frustrating how the TE"RF" narrative regarding second-wave feminism's transmisogyny is reproduced uncritically by motivated gender-conservative actors and their putative opponents alike, and frustrating that despite *Stone Butch Blues'* putative canonization this aspect of its message remains conspicuously buried, even when the TE"RFs" in question both noticed and heavily opposed it! Janice Raymond herself saw fit to attempt to take aim at Feinberg's novel in the 1994 edition of *Transsexual Empire*. *Stone Butch Blues'* gall to humanize and empathize with transsexual women registered to Raymond as an unforgivable transgression, decrying it as "politically disappointing"—inadvertently high praise from one with her politics—and recoiling from its utter rejection of patriarchal gender.

Perhaps that is the one concession we can make to Sister Raymond—she correctly identified where the book's subversive potential lay, an act that seems to be beyond much of the text's modern adherents.

Political disappointment, after all, is not a stranger to *Stone Butch Blues*, less due to its own few shortcomings and more to be attributed to the fandom that has sprung up around it. Feinberg's own brilliance aside, she was not above restating and reifying existing feminist principles and theory. Her keen awareness of the movement's contours infects the story's events, and those with a discerning eye can easily pick out the stances and positions she denounces or adopts, can trace the individual battles of the lesbian-feminist sex wars that Feinberg chooses to correspond on. Her disdain for the TE"RF" line on butchfemmes as "reproducing heterosexuality" is both palpable and humorous, and her utter rejection of the heterosexual regime in plot, theme, and motif is as triumphant as it is spiteful.

That is what *Stone Butch Blues* is—resistance in a hard-bound brick of a text, a rock hewn from the miasma of lesbian-feminist history that recenters its utter and deliberate rejection of gender. It is a battlecry demanding we stare into the mirror and smash the face of the man that patriarchy keeps trying to make us into when it cannot stop us from shedding womanhood's shackles. *Stone Butch Blues* is in many ways a transfeminist text, a historical anomaly raising the banner of transsexual liberation in a time when such a thing was unthinkable—and remains so to this day. Read *Stone Butch Blues*, not because it will tell you exactly how to be a butch, a lesbian, or a transsexual, but because Feinberg's call to action, call to desertion, call to *refusal*, remains every bit as relevant and resonant today as it was when it was released.

Kill the man who wears your face, and tear his flesh apart to reveal your own.

# III

## Interlude

*The following essay is a far more autobiographical piece than I had ever expected to include. It was written at a juncture of great pain, and also introduces some concepts that are key to the rest of my writing.*

# When the Doll Speaks

*Imagine, if you will, the horror one feels, when something that was never meant to have a voice screams.*

## You Left Me To Die

The disproportionately high rates of abuse that trans women suffer—even prior to transition—should not mystify anyone.

Consider, for a moment, how easy it is to isolate a target whose precarity is near-guaranteed. Whether we are vocal or silent about our true identities, whether we are scrabbling for hormones and desperately-needed healthcare or wasting away without them, whether we are actively taking steps to find community with those like us or never breathing a word about what we really are—even to ourselves—a trans woman is always dangling one foot out the door, hoping and praying that *this* time, she can step inside with both feet. Families frequently abandon and disown trans women, and just as frequently exercise more violent options. Exclusion from many economic opportunities and the twin threat of expensive care and inevitable impoverishment is ever-present. All of which pales in comparison to that singular quality which abusers covet over and above all else:

No one believes trans women.

Many factors endemic to transmisogyny underlie this denial of epistemic authority. Plenty of people choose to subscribe to the collective delusion that we occupy a hegemonic male positionality at any point in our lives, an expression of cissexist faith in the naturalization and immutability of sex that does not waver even in the face of contradictory evidence. That we are slandered sometimes with male forms of address is pointed to as a paltry, paper-thin rationalization for ignoring how we are *treated* instead of what we are *called* by those who wish to monster us. The tranny is a "man" only when she can be painted as a brutish, deluded, or perverted one. She is constructed as a *threat* in every instance, one so existential that her very presence justifies all manner of violence against her—all in self-defense, you see.

This is compounded by the reality of the mechanism—trans women are *de*gendered, regarded as some kind of heinous, aberrant, nonhuman *thing* that must never be countenanced, only rectified. Our expressions of pain are manipulations, never sincere. Our wounds are only ever self-inflicted, likely for attention—for who would even want to sully their hands with us? Assaulted—what do you mean? Who could ever want a *thing* like you? You were obviously the one who tricked *them*. How dare you let your misshapen form be inflicted on a poor soul with their hand around your throat? You're lucky he didn't just kill you—and he would have had every right to, too, given what you did.

Degendering dehumanizes us utterly because a patriarchal regime conditions legibility upon gender. Are you imbued with a modicum of agency, your place in society central and venerated and *deified*, the sire and scion of your line? Are you a reproductive asset, a vessel through whom the actual agents of history will perpetuate their marks upon a world forbidden to you?

... Or are you, in fact, something else entirely? Something that is neither citizen nor serf, something that cannot even serve the purpose of incubator, something whose only use can be absorbing as much violence as those around her deem her fit to take?

Are you a still-shambling corpse—dead tranny walking?

I called myself that to my then-girlfriend of just two months, trying to tell her to not get too attached to me, trying to express to her that no matter how hard I tried, I'd realized exactly where all my roads led and she was better off not witnessing my arrival at the destination. That was five years ago, and I've never been more glad to be wrong.

Well.

So far.

## Bury Me Deep

Deepa Mehta's *Fire* notes that Hindi lacks even a word for the term 'lesbian'; it has no concept for the idea of a woman who might love or carnally desire another. Under the harshest contradictions of patriarchies that view women as burdens, as liabilities whose only utility is in ensuring the continuation of male lines, the particularities of a woman's identity become immaterial. A 'lesbian' is a meaningless concept to a culture without any regard for women's interiority, that orients women to a singular purpose whether they are heterosexual, homosexual, asexual, or otherwise: domestic, reproductive, and care work, effectively rendering them indentured servants and a source of uncompensated, undervalued, *feminized* labor. Gender is, ultimately, a labor relation, a set of rationalizations for a social paradigm of exploitation that leans on notions of biodestiny and specific embodiments being *for* specific purposes.

Who or what a woman loves stops mattering; it only matters that she is *used correctly.*

I recommend Adrienne Rich's essay on 'compulsory heterosexuality' because I don't know how to succinctly convey the feeling of panic that settles into my very core when a friend doesn't log in for a few days, or our group simply doesn't hear from them, leading us all to wonder—is this it? Has the regime of heterosexuality *compelled* them finally, press-ganged them back into womanhood and the only purpose women are deemed suited for under it? Friends have told me of fathers who force them to read scripture, who lament their shame and failure at having produced something so 'defective' as a 'daughter' that resists being married off to a man, who insinuate that these 'daughters' are fortunate to still live—that the continuation of their lives is in fact an indescribable act of mercy. We commiserate, we plot, we try to imagine a future untainted by a pall so heavy as to blot out all hope of happiness. Sometimes we succeed.

Just as often, we fail.

While the essay does not mention trans women explicitly, the heterosexual mandate is nevertheless scrawled all over transfeminine histories. In the West, trans women have long been held hostage by medical practitioners—largely men—who demand performances of hyperfemininity from us in exchange for desperately-needed healthcare. This healthcare could and in many places still can be withheld at any time on the basis of arbitrary "psychological evaluations", a well-known euphemism for, to put it bluntly, our *potential fuckability*.

Outside the West, our destinies are even more dire, with the transfeminized being pushed to the absolute margins of society and locked out of the economy at nearly every level. This collectively imposed degendering and impoverishment is frequently justified along theological and cultural lines that credulous anthropologists from Western academies uncritically reproduce, romanticize, and weaponize. Serena Nanda's *Neither Man Nor Woman* holds up South Asia's hijra as objects of macabre Orientalist fascination, waxing rhapsodic about their "social role" as "homosexual male prostitutes" (frequently calling attention to their putative 'maleness' despite the book's own title) and constantly describing their ostracism and suffering with all the detached, casual cruelty of an English children's author. To the Western academic, the subjectivity and activism of transfeminized Third-Worlders is a distant concern next to their rhetorical utility as a 'venerated', vaunted "Third-Sex", casting "primitive yet Enlightened" non-Western cultures as curious gender-practitioners from whom the West has *so much* to learn. All the while, the ways in which Third-Sexed populations like hijra identify with womanhood and organize for legal recognition *as women* are utterly elided; as Serano grimly notes of Nanda's *Gender Diversity* in *Whipping Girl*, the "gender-diversity" of the Orientalized non-Western culture is a sacred cow for many academics who concern themselves with queerness and (supposedly) feminism, a crucial cudgel with which to beat and berate the "medicalized", "Western" transsexual. Transition healthcare that is socio-economically out of reach for many Third World trans women is derided as "imperialism" while the transmisogynistic model of "Third-Sexing", first imposed by our own cultures and then legitimized by *Western* academics, is simply considered scholarship.

Many Westerners, it seems, would happily let my sisters languish without means or care just to reinforce their own worldviews.

Even within this context, I find myself still oddly erased. Afsaneh Najmabadi in *Professing Selves* recounts asking a room full of Iranian transsexuals if any of them were lesbians and receiving blank stares in response, an experience consonant with my two transsexual lesbian friends being asked if they were *best friends* in a Mumbai cafe—by a trans woman. Womanhood is understood to be *for* men, transition understood as a social technology for people who wish to access particular *relations* to *manhood*. Certainly true in the Third World, if not in the West as well, given how much the global transmisogynistic panic fixates on the specter of the rapacious male dressing up in women's garb to sexually exploitative ends. *Lesbianism* remains erased, buried, forbidden to cissexual and transsexual women alike, an untenable identity that many cultures refuse to even acknowledge with contempt.

I have no past, and many would have it that I aspire to no future, either.

Strains of academic feminism exist that consider colonialism to be the genesis of patriarchy, that idealize a prelapsarian pre-patriarchal past that was then tainted by the relentless scourge of worldwide Euro-imperialist hegemony. I do not know how to explain how old the misogyny in Hindu scriptures is, how the history of my people is replete with burned widows and drowned infants and femicidal practices that far predate any British law, how the hijra and khwaja sira were persecuted on the subcontinent long before the Raj, how the 'veneration' of holy men is not actual social capital but rather theological justification for confinement, isolation, and exclusion.

I do not know how to explain to people how many lesbians and trans women and queer people need to flee their abusive families, flee the Third World entirely if they can, because staying where they are means accepting erasure, accepting death, accepting a brutal and brutalized life in the absence of sufficient privileges or luck to shield us from how much our societies abhor those who repudiate the heterosexual-reproductive mandate.

I do not know how to explain to you that our pain matters, that our pain is *real*, and that our pain is important on its own merits and not as rhetorical tools furnished for Westerners in arguments about their own genders and imperialisms and blighted settler-colonial cultures.

My friend would call this *hermeneutical injustice*—a silence and absence of ideas, concepts, and terminology deeper than ripping out tongues or censoring presses can achieve. It is a void, an absence, an utter displacement in time and history because no one like you was ever supposed to exist, and if they did, they were buried *deep*.

I am an aberration, an anomaly, a paradox, and my feminism has always been a struggle to make myself legible—first to myself, then to those both of my culture and not.

It is *strenuously* opposed.

## No Country for Failed Men

My then-girlfriend, now-wife, helped me escape my abusive home and begin my transition.

"Coming out" was not a starting point for me but a grinding halt, the beginning of an arduous five years where after overcoming the hurdles of hermeneutical injustice and learning about transition well into my 20s—and realizing that transition was something *I* personally wanted even later—I was trapped by my circumstances with no access to hormones, no independent finances, and no ability to actually act on my realization. I had consigned myself mentally and emotionally to a slow march to my own dirge, trying to make peace with drowning slowly in a household, society, and nation that would never allow me to be what I truly am. My wife is not merely a life raft, she is the very air in my lungs, oxygen pumped into a failing heart that allows it to beat anew. There is a reason that my first fiction novel is about the liberatory potential of queer love, about finding freedom in each other's arms.

We are not all so lucky.

Luck played a massive part, as did privilege—I do not and will not deny that. Even still, there are many whose impression of Third World migrants is a caricature, a homogenized impression that I am frequently collapsed into. It is undeniable that many legal immigrants to the West are self-selected from among the most affluent of their states, those with the means to successfully navigate the harsh border regimes imposed to keep us in our place. It is also true that diasporic politics often straddle the contradiction between "progressivism" against racialization that targets them in the West and the "conservatism" enjoyed by the comprador classes in the motherland. This does not mean that every one of us can comfortably be smeared as innately reactionary or classist. Many of us from the Third World are displaced in space as well as time, deprived of homeland and history on the basis of our queer identities. Fortunate though I was to find asylum with my wife, it is a happy accident too many of us are denied. Too many of us are not as lucky as I would wish us to be, and the world we inhabit should not be so cruel as to demand we roll the dice to escape our own extinction.

Nor is it truly an escape from the relentless scourge of patriarchy, only a modification of form and character, of going from one state of abjection to another that is less intense in some ways, more intense in others. Moving to the West granted me the 'privilege' of being able to embody my queer identity more openly, of adopting the signifiers and cultural markers of queerness in a language that my tongue was forced to acquire fluency in and a society that enriched itself by feasting upon my people's blood. In exchange I am racialized, a second-class citizen twice over by dint of both my precarious legal status and the *non-whiteness* that is now assigned to me, that now marks me as Other. While I trust my wife completely, it is in fact alarming that my status in this country is utterly dependent on her. Immigrant women from the Third World are frequently abused by partners wielding the precarity of their legal status over their heads. In order to escape one abusive household I've had to make myself susceptible to abuse in another, have had to rely even more heavily on goodwill and fortune.

All to exist openly in a society that still reviles me and those like me and whose wealth is founded upon the untold and uncountable atrocities that constitute my nation's past. I recall having a panic attack the first time my wife took me to Cambridge. I could see bloodstains on the flagstones.

That precarity has been compounded by my sudden unemployability. After being unable to secure adequate healthcare for my disability on the NHS—I did not even bother attempting to seek transition-related healthcare—I was forced to resort to the expensive yet still-flagging private sector and was unable to retain my job. Since then, despite an increase in qualifications, and despite no longer needing sponsorship, I find myself unable to secure more than first-round interviews, whereas a fictional man with my legal name had frequently managed to get to the third round for positions that now turned their noses up at me. Transition does many things, and one of the things it does best is erode fortunes, no matter how robust. We have been subsisting on my wife's disability benefits.

Despite this, I am still in a more secure position than most of my kin, if only through the generosity and acceptance of my in-laws. I still do my best to help others and I make a point of not asking for help myself when so many more aren't as fortunate as I have been. My life hangs by a thread, but at least that thread is golden; I worry greatly for those without the 'privilege'.

So I stand, cleft from two cultures that revile me, one whose abuses I had to flee from and one whose abuses I have no choice but to subject myself to. My feminist theory is explicitly from this perspective, adrift in these currents, where I do my best to shout over the din and give name to the ways in which my identity, my experiences, and my epistemic authority are all erased to serve others' ends.

Often, I feel alone. Until recently, I didn't feel that quite so keenly—had thought I had found comrades and sisters and fellow-travelers, people who understood. People who wouldn't subject me to the particular process of dehumanizing invalidation I have grown so used to in spaces both online and off.

I know better now.

## I Tried

It started as a small Discord server for those who enjoyed my writing.

Author Discords are relatively banal, informal spaces. A few of my friends have modest ones, with some having truly gigantic ones, but I never expected mine to be particularly sizeable. My fiction debut had been a modest success by indie standards but it still did not mean any degree of significant reach. Several people hopped on when I shared the invite link on social media, and several of my friends did as well.

Predictably, perhaps, my Author Discord did not remain an Author Discord for long. I enjoy writing fiction and I enjoy producing the sorts of narratives I personally wished I could have seen growing up—narratives that regard lesbians and trans women as whole people with complexity and internality. Even so, my true passion has always been feminism, so much so that it undergirds even the fiction I write, and informs the way I construct narrative arcs and address themes. More and more people asked to join not because of my self-published book, but because in the process of socializing and interacting with friends on the server, I could not stop discussing feminism and feminist theory. The channels about my writing languished while the singular 'feminism' channel expanded, and the server slowly began to look more and more like a *transfeminist* forum. Eventually, it somehow acquired a reputation as one too, even as I still mostly considered it an informal, social arena.

An interesting dynamic that cropped up was the sheer number of demands that were placed upon me by those in the server, while a bizarre degree of resentment and vitriol began to swell amidst some who were not. Strange accusations of exclusivity, reactionary sentiment, and imagined goings-on were fielded publicly, while privately the space remained an avenue for me to organize watch parties, speak to my friends scattered across time zones, and discuss the feminist theory I was familiar with and that I wanted to write. Over time, more and more was asked of me with regard to formalizing the pursuit of feminist work, feminist readings, feminist discussions, feminist writing—all of which was expected to fall upon me. The demands were many, the offers to assist few.

I found myself, once again, at the nexus of simultaneous monstering and pedestalization. Those who felt slighted for reasons I cannot fathom felt comfortable declaring me a fascist (due to my nation's current regime—which I had to flee) or accusing me of uncritically regurgitating Second-Wave orthodoxy without actually pointing to my writing or my work to substantiate such claims. The 'ontological immaturity' and 'conservative character' of lesbian feminism were held forth as a charge that I was viciously berated for repudiating. Queer people from the first world—some trans, some even trans women themselves—searched for a justification to fit their distrust or disagreement. I could not be someone with a differing ideological approach or a unique perspective—there *had* to be something about me that rendered me secretly a bad actor, an evil radfem with ill intent and malicious designs, all for my nefarious goal of taking a materialist approach to transfeminist theorizing, explicitly from my point of view as a trans lesbian who survived Third World patriarchy.

A white trans woman told my girlfriend privately that I was the "angriest woman on the internet" and a "rage demon". It is not the first time brown women like me have been painted as uncaring aggressors from whose rampaging excesses more-delicate women need to be safeguarded.

Meanwhile, I was being asked to do more and more in the server, things I *wanted* to do but found difficult to keep up with in the face of bad-faith racialized attacks from my own "community". The need for engagement with more strains of feminism was repeatedly stressed to me, without which could I really speak on topics pertinent to my own life and the lives of women like me? I was asked to know everything and share my expertise; folks would not so much as arrange discussions they wanted to have of their own volition but would ask me to organize and prioritize and plan at their behest.

Not once was it ever asked whether my work could have merit without existing in conversation with every other strain of feminism, several of which treat the oppression of Third World women as a rhetorical abstraction. It was taken as a given that anything I had to say could not possibly have value on its own merits, that my perspective as a trans lesbian from the Third World could not possibly stand on its own. Being in conversation with other schools of thought is integral to scholarship, but I was not asked to be in conversation with others—I was told in no uncertain terms that my own work would not be adequately progressive, would somehow fall prey to reactionary tendency, unless I deprioritized drawing on my own culture's patriarchy and my own empirical observations and subordinated my own life's work to the prevailing orthodoxy.

I was, frankly, being asked to deny my own epistemic authority, specifically to center and engage with work that has long neglected women like me.

That is, ultimately, the rub. Due to the erasure of women like me—transfeminized, lesbian, of the Third World—due to the epistemic injustice we are subject to, it is easy for others to define me, to construct a phantasmatic apparition whose sins I can be held accountable for. Neither those who denounced me nor those who sought to extract more and more labor from me truly saw me as a person, only something to instrumentalize, to repurpose to their own ends.

I am a brown trans dyke from the global south, and women like me are not supposed to speak for ourselves.

So I acquiesced and, deleting the server and my online presence, I fell silent.

## Feel My Pain

Because women like me are reduced to tools for others to exploit, it is easy to vilify us when we do not allow ourselves to be exploited. My country is the world's sweatshop and brothel, an impoverished nation riddled with contradictions and harsh conservative regimes. My sisters are exploited by their "fellow" men as my nation is exploited by the hegemonic worldwide economic order, avenues for cheap labor both. When we are recognized, it is an Orientalized recognition, an exotified caricature of our practices or cuisine or women. Even the transmisogyny of my society, that so brutalizes transfeminized populations, is considered a fascinating and core aspect of our culture held up beyond critique.

So when we do not follow a Westernized script as Third World women, or a patriarchal script as transfeminized women, we are treated as broken dolls, as things contravening our intended purpose, fit only to vent upon and discard. Our lives become a repeating pattern of trying to find those who will not subject us to this, who will see us as people and not resources to mine. We are constantly threatened with degendering, bestialization, sexualization, demonization, and easily-achieved ostracism and social isolation from communities that only ever valued us as rhetorical mouthpieces and grew displeased at our temerity to express and insist upon our own viewpoints.

All of which is an inseparable miasmic slop that I cannot disentangle any more than I could part the sea. I cannot tell you where the racialization ends and the transmisogyny begins, which bit was in opposition to me as a lesbian feminist who refused to let her identity be disparaged and which bit was just because I was a Third Worlder speaking out of turn and refusing to let Westerners romanticize my "gender-enlightened culture". None of it, no single aspect of me was acceptable to those who would prefer that my existence hew to a simple narrative, or otherwise fade away entirely.

Which I *refuse* to do.

I do not know how to explain to you that my pain matters, that I spend every moment agonizing over how best to draw people's attention to the plights of queer women they would much rather forget. I don't know how to explain to you that patriarchy is not a uniquely Eurocolonial invention, that my sisters and foremothers have been sacrificed on the altar of manhood for aeons and will continue to be unless it is *stopped*. I do not know how to explain to you that the West, whether protagonist or antagonist, wishes to be the absolute center of history, and it is decidedly *not*.

So I won't bother.

I will keep working, I will keep speaking, and I will scream and scream and scream until I am heard, or until someone has the guts to silence me for good. What I have to say *matters*. Undoing the erasure of women like me *matters*. We are not your dolls, we are not your props. Our. Pain. *Matters*.

There is a future for people like me, and you will simply have to live in it.

# IV

# Part Three: Epistemicide

*A dissection of the deep-rooted and far-reaching history of transmisogyny in academia, cultural studies, and feminism itself.*

# "Sex is Real": The Core of Gender-Conservative Anxiety

One of the most common refrains you will hear from those who are discomfited by the existence of transsexual people is "sex is real!", or "biological sex is real!" if they're attempting to sound particularly scientific in their blunt assertions. There is a lot encoded into this three-word shibboleth, imbuing a near-tautological statement with oodles of political baggage: that the reality of sex somehow stands in contradiction to the existence of transsexual people, that transsexual people are allegedly disputing and denying the existence of something so fundamental as (biological!) sex, that believing in transsexualism so flies in the face of "common sense" that sex-essentialism is by *reductio ad absurdum* the only reasonable, rational, *natural* position to take.

It's a routine we've all seen many, many times.

As always, there is a response to this assertion that is *trivial*, that takes the claims of "sex is real" at face value and contradicts some of its basic inferences: that transsexual people, who pursue hormone replacement therapy and surgical affirmation, are *painfully* aware of the 'reality' of sex, are perhaps more aware of sex's tangible impositions on one's life and body than those who are not transsexual. One can even attempt to challenge some of the more overtly political implications of that oft-shouted exclamation and say that the 'reality' of sex does not contradict transsexual existence in the slightest, that these are not ideologically or politically antagonistic concepts. To do so is to miss the true philosophical undergirding of this slogan and other related ones (such as "sex matters!"). Despite there being so few words here, many people still somehow focus on the wrong ones. Crucially, the entire statement cannot be sufficiently unpacked without taking a close look at the many assumptions, worldviews and motivations behind the gender-conservative's use of the word *sex* itself.

When a gender-conservative uses the term *sex*, they mean *naturalized, patriarchal, essentialist* ideas of sex. When they say "sex is real" or "sex matters", what they actually mean is that sex is *determined at birth* and *immutable*.

To be clear, while the fevered repetition of these mantras in order to reinforce one's belief and dispel any challenges to the Patriarchal Faith is unique to the most radicalized and bigotry-motivated, even putative 'allies' who style themselves as progressive or liberal in terms of social issues and 'transgender politics' struggle with these anxieties. Popular understandings and illustrations dichotomize sex and gender entirely, constructing a worldview where *gender* is a social phenomenon and a malleable identity one can declare, claim, or brand as one sees fit, while sex remains this *biological reality* observed at birth, untouchable and unchangeable, safely ensconced in a realm beyond the mere *social*. Clearly, it is not only the ones who openly declare their opposition to transsexual existence who draw comfort from this idea of naturalized sex.

Social constructs are hardly divorced from tangibility, of course—readers may recall that meters measure actual distance, even if the choice of exactly what length to declare as a 'meter' was arbitrary and had to be agreed upon. *Consensus* rules human reality, often much more than even tangible observation—trans women would otherwise not be so often asked to take pregnancy tests during check-ups. *Sexing* is in fact far from a process limited to birth or confined to medical experts; it occurs *constantly*, regularly as a part of social dynamics and moving through the world. People do not in fact karyotype each other or perform genital inspections before deciding whether someone, based on their presentation and appearance, should be treated as a man, woman, or something rather more ambiguous and *queer*. Most of us think that certain presentations and visible characteristics correspond to certain genital configurations, karyotypes, reproductive capacities, anatomical realities, and even (if we're attuned to patriarchal social norms) certain dispositions, attitudes, preferences, occupations, income levels, and so on and so forth. Sex is thus not simply socially constructed in this sense—where we have decided specific characteristics correspond to specific biological qualities about a person, an inference that might not even be true for non-transsexual people—but is socially constructed in an *essentializing* way, where it is fashioned as an intrinsic quality that is imbued with specific social meanings of autonomy, inferiority, and *social status*.

That is, after all, what it means for *gender* and *heterosexuality* to be *regimes*—social sex becomes an indication of a certain social status.

Here, the true anxiety of the gender-conservative—whether spitting, frothing ideologue or unquestioning bystander—is laid bare. The rigid authoritarianism of conservatives does not simply enshrine certain social norms, but always seeks to naturalize them, to uphold them as truths that are beyond the reach of society's capricious influences. There is no better mechanism by which one can validate traditional norms than by holding them to be *unimpeachable*, natural in some divine, ontological way that precedes politics, that *precedes society*. Gender can be made-up bunk now, since all the half-crazed transsexuals go around claiming it is—but *sex*, don't you dare deny the reality of sex! Sex is real! Sex matters! There are two sexes, *pee-pee* and *hoo-ha*, and they determine everything important about you at birth!

Supremacist logics and conservative mindsets love rules, even when the rules aren't clearly slanted in their favor (but of course, especially when they are). Whether through upholding society's *natural state* or collaborating with the social regime's beneficiaries, conservatives see ironclad rules as way to *secure order*—another euphemism, which conceals a desire for society to be *regular, predictable, deterministic,* and therefore comfortable in a way only something static and routine can be. The most terrifying prospect is that the rules are arbitrary, that they were set up in a particular way to benefit particular people, and are subject to *change*, to *disruption* and *destabilization*.

The core of conservative existential terror is the idea that social norms, even deeply-held, highly-embedded ones, could be questioned, altered, transformed—*transcended*. Even if they are someone whom the rules don't currently benefit, what if the changed rules benefit them even less? A cruel, tyrannical god may harm you, abuse you, but at least if you understand his rules, you can play by them, you can attempt to curry favor. What could be more frightening than a world with no gods and no masters?

What is more terrifying than the idea that you could define what matters on your own, autonomous terms, without anyone telling you what is sacred and what is profane?

Sex is real. The concept of sex they learned as babies, as schoolchildren, as participants in a patriarchal society *must be real*, because the alternative—they don't know how to contemplate the alternative. If they live in a world where sex is *mutable*, where someone can cross gender lines and for all intents and purposes interface with society as a different sex than the one coercively imposed upon them at birth, then they live in a world where some of the basic, fundamental beliefs they hold are in fact more arbitrary and underminable than they thought possible. It would destroy the very foundations of patriarchy and make them question everything they thought they knew about sex and the social regime built upon it.

They wouldn't know what to do in a world where sex doesn't matter.

# The Transmisogyny Bible: A Critical Dissection

*The Transsexual Empire* began its life as a religious studies dissertation under the supervision of Mary Daly. The book itself is dedicated to her and cites her liberally, if her fingerprints all over the text's structure and argumentation were insufficiently obvious for a casual reader. Given that Janice Raymond herself left the Sisters of Mercy, this makes the book a rather fascinating artifact, a labor undertaken by two former Roman Catholics whose personal disagreements with the faith do not appear to have led to a critical re-examination of their own philosophies, ontologies, or modes of thinking.

Indeed, *The Transsexual Empire* is a remarkably Catholic book—in *spirit* if not in letter. Very amusingly, about a paragraph into the book's original introduction, Janice Raymond concedes that transsexuals do, in fact, change their sex. She cattily refers to trans women as "male-to-constructed-female", ensconcing pronouns within scare quotes in an effort to 'expose' the artificiality of the Transsexual's entire Be-ing, but in the process admits that through hormones, surgeries or some combination thereof, the transsexual does indeed undergo physiological changes and processes that reconstitute her bodily. It is an amusing admission precisely because of how bizarrely far Raymond goes in constructing an artificial barrier between the supposed mirage of transsexual womanhood when transposed against the "real thing", as though patriarchy subjects us all to karyotyping prior to determining whether we ought to be subject to misogyny. For not even a page into the work can Janice Raymond pretend that gender is not social; her answer to this is to ignore the social entirely, to dive into chromosomes and pharmaceutical conspiracies and Wholeness of Spirit, amidst other assorted esoterica that is meant to evoke the Frankenstinian nature of trans womanhood, to monster us in a remarkably literal manner.

It is an approach that will be emulated for decades.

There is a sense in which attempting to fact-check the book, to subject it to any sort of rigorous analysis is in and of itself an exercise in futility; contradictions abound, unaddressed and straightforward to highlight with little effort. Raymond asserts that transsexual women avail of surgery at much higher rates than transsexual men, but selectively focuses on SRS to do so; looking at top surgery would easily invert that figure. Raymond asserts that transsexual women are uniformly heterosexual, traditionalist and right-wing, invested in "stereotypes of womanhood", then herself cites a transsexual woman who explains (one imagines slowly, while enunciating) that the medical industry itself mandates specific behaviors, outlooks and worldviews from transsexuals before permitting them to access transition care, resulting in a highly self-selected group. Rather than reckoning with the horrors of such gatekeeping and surveillance, or highlighting the extent to which transsexual women must perform a patriarchal womanhood for mostly-male doctors on pain of being barred from the medicine they require, Raymond is only too happy to damn the lot, to blame transsexuals for the sins of the very people abusing and controlling them.

Given her clear disdain for heterosexualism, does lesbian feminist Janice Raymond exult at the discovery of transsexuals who are unapologetically queer? Of course not: her greatest, most pointed ire is reserved for those transsexuals she considers perversions of a supposed lesbian purity. *Sappho by Surgery* is her most vicious, caustic chapter by far, a tirade against a specific transsexual woman whom she deems unworthy of participating in a radical feminist collective—against the very collective's wishes and defenses of said woman! Janice Raymod boldly and bravely sticks her opinion where it is not wanted, declaring Sandy Stone an "invasive" presence in feminist spaces with no hint of irony and less self-awareness. She had, in fact, sent a draft of this chapter to Olivia Records in 1976, kicking off an escalating series of hostilities, campaigns and boycott threats before Stone voluntarily left the collective. Stone's transgression was daring to share the expertise she'd accrued in a male-dominated music industry with a woman-only feminist collective, an act that Raymond could not forgive due to Stone's Original Sin of maleness and "male energy".

In the book's 1994 edition, Raymond deemed Leslie Feinberg worthy of similar treatment in the subsection of a new introduction that she provocatively titled *The Transgendered Lesbian*. In it she excoriates firebrand, socialist and actual feminist Leslie Feinberg for daring to conclude in her most popular work, *Stone Butch Blues*, that lesbians can and ought to find a sense of kinship and solidarity with transsexual women. Even a decade and a half after the book's initial publication, that sense of petty vindictiveness that so pervades Raymond's writing is intact, cementing once and for all how the facade of feminist scholarship is invoked to provide a paper-thin veneer for her own personal grievances, against transsexuality writ large if not against specific activists whose politics she has the gall to judge as lacking.

For that is what *The Transsexual Empire* ultimately is—one "ex"-Catholic's ground-down axes masquerading as substantive feminist critique. The book can hardly stand on its own merits, positing a wide-ranging 'male conspiracy' to bilk poor, conflicted and confused transsexuals by subjecting them to unnecessary medicalization instead of providing them with the (conversion) therapy they truly need to be at peace. Such a fiery accusation, attacking the very foundations of the hyper-capitalist pharmaceutical industry, meets a rather watery end in the tome's own pages, where Raymond notes the hostility with which psychiatrists, sexologists and medical gatekeepers regard transsexual women, rejecting the majority as unworthy of the care they request and require. An endeavor to turn transsexuality into a new medical-industrial cash cow is somewhat undercut when those administering that healthcare themselves frequently turn away perfectly willing and paying clients. Perhaps this is a form of capitalist exploitation with which we are—to this day—unfamiliar.

On what does the book's thesis ultimately rest, then? The answer is "not very much". Commensurate with Raymond's hyperfocus on chromosomes as the true determiner of one's sex over the various phenotypical and endocrinal changes she tacitly admits transsexual women undergo, Raymond insists that the transsexual's ultimate crime is a violation of our own bodily integrity. The phrase "God's design" is absent on the page but very much present between the lines, as Raymond strains to describe the severity of transsexual women's crimes against our Selves. A similar line of reasoning led her to polemicize against mifepristone in *Misconceptions, Myths and Morals*, demonstrating quite comprehensively how Raymond's conception of bodily *integrity* has nothing to do with bodily *autonomy*. There is a "higher power" that Janice Raymond refuses to name but who must be considered when making decisions about one's own flesh, to ascertain whether it is truly the right choice or whether one is better served by healing one's spiritual sickness over fixating on worldly matters.

Sister Raymond, it would appear, never quite left that convent.

Despite this—despite the flimsiness of the text to which most modern institutional transphobia can be traced, a happy ending remains elusive. For the sad truth is that *The Transsexual Empire* never needed to be rigorous, never needed to be well-formulated, immaculately researched and coherently argued. It simply needed to exist. It simply needed to be a shameless, incisive and polemical text that accuses transsexual existence itself of being "rape" while ignoring the rampant sexual abuse of transsexual women both within the medical industry and without. The book's existence was enough, providing ready citations to motivated actors whose disgust and disinclination towards transsexuals needed no sound reasoning and the most threadbare of justifications. To wit: the book's epilogue is not a summary or a conclusion or a retread of its arguments but a *prescription*, a list of concrete actions that must be taken to curb the burgeoning transsexual threat. It gives me no joy to report that Janice Raymond's marching orders to limit the number of trans clinics and throttle transsexual existence at the policy level has seen wide adoption.

Even that observation undermines the book's *cultural* impact. Raymond constructs a pharmaceutical specter in order to exorcize it with what she believes to be the *true* curative for transsexuality: conversion therapy. The transsexual is a sick individual whose *mind and spirit* need healing more than her body. If she perceives herself to have no place in a patriarchal society, she must be treated by encouraging her to view herself as a gender non-conforming individual rather than allowing her to *mutilate* herself with the healthcare she desperately requires. Raymond views transsexuality as *regressive*, as caving to patriarchal society's narrow definitions of "man" and "woman"; the solution is to carve out a unique path so that the individual becomes someone who *fights* patriarchal edicts instead of *conforming* to them. The fact that seizing one's biodestiny, defying the declared immutability of sex, rejecting the enforcement of sexual difference, and embracing transsexual existence is in-and-of-itself a cataclysmic undermining of patriarchy's very foundations, is, *naturally*, not remarked upon.

Such is the legacy of *The Transsexual Empire*: Decades after its publication, this view of transition and transsexuality is practically the liberal-feminist, 'progressive' consensus. Academics as respected as Judith Butler have trotted out the line that transition is "conformist". Worse still, the idea that trans people do not change their *sex*, only their *gender*, is now commonplace in queer-liberal discourses. Macabre models such as the "gender unicorn" and "genderbread person" helpfully perpetuate a model of sex whereby its immutability is never challenged, where despite whatever changes trans people make to our bodies, "no one is claiming that trans people actually change their sex". The freaks are simply playing pretend, well-informed "allies" chortle amongst each other, and the polite thing to do is to humor them while remembering that their *birth sex*, their *natal assignment* is, of course, inescapable.

And so goes the cruelest punchline of the joke that is *The Transsexual Empire*: the modern liberal-feminist progressive, so enlightened on queer and trans issues, is now less willing to admit that transsexual people do in fact change our sex than Janice Raymond was in her Transmisogyny Bible.

# The Third Sex

*"The Gender Binary" is a misnomer; gender has always been a hierarchy.*

## Introduction: This Machine Builds Fascists

Consider a mechanism whose sole function is to classify all inputs it receives as one of two categories: One and Zero. The inputs, it must be said, vary greatly in temperament, expression, embodiment, internality, and so on, but that isn't as much of a hurdle for the machine as it seems. It has been programmed with a few simple lines of code that enable it to differentiate between Ones and Zeroes within acceptable margins of tolerance. Ones tend to look and behave like *this*, Zeroes tend to be like *that*. These truisms are crude, simplistic, and even reductive, true, but they *work*. As such, the machine chugs on, happily reducing complex inputs to a blunt binary classification, its delivery-day code having been deemed "good enough".

Of course, there is still the matter of how the machine should behave when its schema fails, when it is presented with inputs that do indeed prove to be too ambiguous to easily classify. For however high the correlation between traits, sometimes a specimen that simply defies easy categorization will confound its decision-making, often enough to pose a problem. Does the code need to be updated? Almost certainly, but legacy code is a stubborn thing, mired in dependencies and versioning faff, deeply resistant to the most perfunctory of edits. Too many now rely on this iteration of the machine, on this particular instantiation of its logic, and it is almost universally agreed that any changes are best handled downstream—at least, among those with the power to change it.

The machine and its users are thus forced to consider: In the case of an "error", a "mistake", so to speak, is it better to classify something as a One or a Zero?

Well, that's an easy enough decision. The Ones, you see, are quite important, are believed to play a rather critical role in the affairs the machine oversees. The Zeroes ... sure, they're certainly important too, in their own way, in the way everything worth categorizing is—but the Ones! It's really all about the Ones. You can't quite go around just calling anything a One, you have to be *certain*.

So the module is attached and business proceeds without interruption. The machine spits out Ones and Zeroes like it's supposed to, like it always has and supposedly always will, a binary system choosing between two options. Yet, anyone who knows a little too much about its inner workings is perfectly aware that the machine's neat bifurcation isn't all that neat. Truthfully, the machine has *three* outputs: One, Zero (with a degree of confidence), and "NULL". It's just that the exceptions are caught and sorted into the Zero-category, because that method of handling the machine's limitations still keeps things running smoothly. It's not much of an issue at all, and there's no real need to examine the machine any further.

No need to pay attention to the way its NULL exceptions keep rising in volume.

No need to examine it for any shortcomings, oversights ... or any weaknesses.

# Part One: Neither Correct Nor Considerate

# The Contradiction

*Neither Man Nor Woman* is an ethnography of India's hijra, undertaken by anthropologist Serena Nanda. It is a text that has, in many ways, proved foundational to the West's understanding of so-called "Third Genders" and "Third Sexes" in non-Western cultures, providing an academic basis for the consideration of gendered expansivity and putatively non-binary gender systems the world over. Certainly, it is difficult to find a more-cited work on the hijra, and Nanda can perhaps be credited with setting the terms on which the Western academy—if not the West at large—has been made aware of hijra life.

Despite its own title, Serena Nanda's *Neither Man Nor Woman* states in the very second sentence that South Asia's hijras are "a religious community of **men who dress and act like women**." (Emphasis mine.) It is a contradiction the book is either unaware of or uninterested in addressing, since it is repeatedly reasserted and reinforced throughout the remainder of the text. Therein, Nanda—a cis woman—takes a look at this community through the eyes of someone unfamiliar with the Indian cultural context, learning about them through both observation and testimony. The resulting ethnography triangulates and emphasizes several crucial details: that the hijra are a "religious cult" of "ascetics" centered around the worship of the goddess Bahuchara Mata; that hijras are often present at rituals and celebrations, usually weddings, to perform dances and bless the newlyweds with fertility and a firstborn son; that they grow their hair long, wear women's clothes and assume an "exaggerated and garish femininity"; and that they form their own community structure, living on the margins of Indian society.

Often, the undercurrent of the author's lurid fascination with the hijra bubbles to the surface, such as when she describes witnessing the results of the hijras' "emasculation operation"—her needlessly grandiose euphemism for castration. Rhapsodic, meandering elaborations on Hindu myths and spirituality are jarringly interspersed with discussions of the hijras' "sexual impotence", their role as "homosexual male prostitutes", and their "grotesque, sexually suggestive parody of feminine behavior". Nanda seems morbidly fixated on resolving what seems to her the central paradox of hijra existence, namely their supposed religious asceticism juxtaposed against their involvement in sex work, or their desire for "husbands"—a term that always appears in quotation marks within the text. She maps their kinship structures, details their lives, and reproduces first-person accounts, all while insisting on their "maleness", frequently contrary to their own words.

Why, then, is the book *Neither Man Nor Woman* instead of *Emasculated Homosexual Religious Ascetics*? Nanda repeatedly alludes to the concept of a "Third Gender" or "Third Sex" without any degree of rigor, without explicating what such a term may connote. The belief in two biological, opposing, and non-overlapping "sexes" is confidently touted as "Western", but the basis for that differentiation is never unearthed or examined, nor any rationalizations provided for how the West's social strictures may deviate from those of societies with alleged "Third Sexes". The concept itself rests on shaky ground and the book seems content to—ironically—allow the reader's existing notions of "sex" to dictate the meaning they derive from this construction.

Chapter Two is the closest that Nanda comes to actually dissecting these concepts in the consecutive subsections *Hijras As "Not Men"* and *Hijras As "Not Women"*. These are fascinating subheadings, given that the *Hijras As "Not Men"* subsection contains a rather thorough listing of their similarities with *women*. Nanda herself notes just how much hijras stress that they are *not men* when discussing themselves, which makes her word choices throughout the book all the more confounding. For all of her disavowals of the West's "rigid binary" that is purportedly unable to conceptualize a "third sex", she is steadfast in tethering hijras to maleness, perhaps to offer herself as a shining example of the limited Western imaginary.

It is Nanda's attempt to rhetorically distance hijras from womanhood, however, that proves to be the most revealing. Ignoring her own reporting of how hijras travel in "ladies" compartments on the trains and "periodically demand" to be counted as women in the census, she begins *Hijras As "Not Women"* by affirming that hijras behave in manners "in opposition to the Hindu ideal of demure and restrained femininity". What follows is an amusing account of all the behaviors that set hijra apart from True Womanhood: "dancing in public", "coarse and abusive speech or gestures", smoking hookah or cigarettes, and openly exhibiting a "shameless" vulgarity that no "real" Hindu woman would indulge. No doubt many Indian housewives would be edified to learn how trivial it is to change sex, or how frequently they've done so in the process of haggling for cheaper vegetables.

Less amusing is the invocation of 18th-century legal codes that required hijra to wear men's turbans or coats to "distinguish" themselves as not-women—as though decrees of state are an adequate source for settling the question of hijra identity—preceding the passage that lays Nanda's ideological investments bare. She recounts two stories told to her that, she claims, serve as "testimony to the hijra view of themselves as 'not women', *at least not real women*". (Emphasis mine). Both stories are reproduced here in full, with certain portions italicized to highlight them:

> *See, two people got into a fight, a man and a hijra.* The hijra said, "I am a lady", and the man said, "No, you are not." The fight went so long that they went to the magistrate. The magistrate said, "I agree, you look like a woman, you act like a woman, but I'll ask you a simple question—can you give birth to a baby? If that is not possible, then you don't win." *The hijra answered, no, she could not give birth to a baby, so the magistrate said, "You are only a hijra, you are not a woman."*
>
> In Ajmer, in North India, there is a holy place that belongs to the hijras. It is called Baba Darga, and it is on top of a hill. One time, during Urs [a Muslim festival], many people were going up the hill to pay respects to Baba. One hijra was also there. She saw a lady with four children and offered to carry one or two of them. The lady became very angry and told the hijra, "You are a hijra, so don't touch my children." This made the hijra feel very sad, so she asked Baba for his blessings for a child of her own. But she only asked for a child and didn't ask Baba to bring the child out. The pregnancy went on for ten months, and her stomach became very bloated. She went to the doctor's but they didn't want to perform an operation [Caesarean section] on her. Eventually she couldn't stand the weight any longer so she prayed to the Baba to redeem her from this situation. But Baba could only grant her the boon, he could not reverse it. When the hijra felt she could stand it no more, she found a sword at the darga [Muslim shrine] and slit herself open. She removed the child and placed it on the ground. The child died and the hijra also died. Now at this darga prayers are performed to this hijra

*and the child and then to the Baba.*

What stands out the most is the startling lack of empathy. Rather than meditating on these tales as exemplary of the hijra's struggle for legibility as women against a society that structurally and legally denies them that, Nanda is happy to cite them as "evidence" of hijras reaffirming their own degendering. Of the hijra who narrated the second story, Nanda has this to say:

> *"This story reveals an ambivalence: On the one hand, it expresses the wish of some hijras to have a child, yet on the other hand acknowledges its impossibility. The death of the hijra and the child suggests that hijras cannot become women—in the most fundamental sense of being able to bear a child—and that they are courting disaster to attempt something so contrary to their nature. Meera, the hijra who told me this story, was convinced it was true. She had many times expressed to me her wish for a child and said that she had read in a magazine that in America doctors would help people like her have babies. The other hijras sitting with us laughed at this suggestion."*

Leaving aside the casual cruelty for the moment, we are able to glean an equivocation that Nanda presents as neutral, but is very much ideological: the *equation of womanhood with gestational capacity*. Just as the book fails to comment upon Indian society's repression of the hijra, or the hermeneutical injustice inherent to denying their self-understanding in favor of forcing them to accept a stigmatized categorization, it also neglects to consider how holding reproductive capacity as *the* essential characteristic of womanhood is thoroughly patriarchal. Nanda does not meaningfully inquire how such a view, deeply entrenched in Indian society, might impact even cis (or *real*) women, an incuriosity that leads to the book's clearest example of cultural illiteracy.

## The Barren

We return to chapter one, where the author discusses her observations of a hijra troop performing at wedding ceremonies. Ignoring how eagerly she refers to this as a "grotesque, sexually suggestive parody of feminine behavior"—her predisposition towards treating hijra identity as simple mimesis is well-established—let us instead consider an interesting tidbit, buried under the overly-florid attempts to do the performances justice. On page four, the following sentence betrays Nanda's motivated reasoning:

> "Some more orthodox families do not allow the bride to be present in the courtyard with the hijras, however, believing that the hijras' infertility will contaminate the girl and keep her from having a son."

She revisits this on page six:

> "Thus, the stout, middle-class matrons who are so amused by the hijras' performances, and who may even pity them as tragic, hermaphroditic figures, also have an underlying anxiety about them. As mentioned earlier, this is translated into a taboo of orthodox Hindus that the hijras should not touch, or even see, a new bride, so that their impotence will not contaminate her reproductive potential."

Here, the author uses "impotence" rather than "infertility", a word choice that firmly calls to mind Nanda's repeated assertions of the hijra's 'castrated manhood'. It is interesting primarily because anyone familiar with the Indian cultural context would be able to tell you that this superstition, this belief that infertility can spread, is not one that is usually applied to *men*.

*Baanjh* is the term used for an infertile woman, which translates rather directly to *barren*. Indian society's reduction of women to their role of broodmare, mere vessels to further a man's line, ensures that women who cannot fulfill this role face harsh stigma and censure. 'Barren' women are reduced almost to the state of untouchables, considered to be carrying 'bad energy' that could 'infect' and bring misfortune upon those they interact with. Their treatment calls to mind the reality of societies with intense patriarchal contradictions and demonstrates how women are accorded no humanity, no internality, and no autonomy outside of their reproductive roles.

It is telling that the book makes nothing of this observation, going so far as to reify the hijras' supposed maleness, because the author does not understand that this is a belief firmly rooted in viewing the hijra as *barren women*. There is no clearer demonstration of how Nanda is clearly working backward from a conclusion, rather than investigating the conditions of an abjectified population and reporting on their lives in a conscientious, sensitive manner. Her fixation is given primacy over evidence of how hijra are viewed and treated similarly to women who cannot fulfill their reproductive roles—evidence that she presents herself, without even understanding its implications.

All of which begs the question—what end do these omissions serve? Why, ultimately, is a cultural anthropologist invested in disregarding the affinity that the hijra display for legible womanhood in favor of propping them up as an "institutionalized third gender", filling the 'social role' of "homosexual male prostitute"?

## The Omission

The first time in this book that Serena Nanda discusses transsexuality in-depth is in chapter *ten*.

> *"Unlike the alternative gender roles found in other cultures, the transsexual in American culture is not viewed as a third, or alternative, gender. Rather, transsexualism has been defined in such a way as to reinforce our cultural construction of both sex and gender as invariably dichotomous."*

Once more, Nanda places rhetorical distance between the hijra and a category that they would appear to bear more than a passing resemblance to—transsexuals, in this case. Here she espouses strangely familiar rhetoric of transsexuals as *medicalized*, regarding transsexuality as a by-product of the 'Euro-American medical complex' attempting to preserve the European understanding of gender as dichotomous. Transsexuality, she laments, is popularly understood as a liminal state between the two genders, leaving no room for gender-expansivity or third-sexes. While she does accurately convey the role medical practitioners played in enforcing gender norms upon transsexuals, allowing care only to those they deemed sufficiently conformist, Nanda nonetheless laments that the greatest champions of this "liminal view" of transsexuality were transsexuals themselves. Her characteristic inability to notice the compromises a hyperscrutinized population must make with the society repressing them thus once more rears its head.

Central to Nanda's distinction between the Western transsexual and the Indian hijra is the issue of, as she puts it, "medicalization". Regressive transsexuals do not challenge binaristic notions of Euro-American gender and seek 'medicalization' to cross from one sex to the other without disrupting the gendered hegemony, while noble third-sexed individuals inhabit an *expansive* cultural role, challenging the Western understanding of dichotomous sex on a fundamental level.

Robust as this thesis is, it would certainly face issues if any hijra were to express a desire for 'medicalization'—as one of Nanda's *own informants* did, candidly discussing her hormonal treatments and desires for 'normative' womanhood.

Later scholarship, such as Gayatri Reddy's *With Respect to Sex*, touches upon many hijras' desire for secondary sexual characteristics corresponding to womanhood, with Reddy expressing concern about how they consume many birth control pills daily, or seek out unprescribed hormonal injections. Neglecting to mention the hijras' desire for "medicalization" would be understandable if Nanda never encountered any hijra who trusted her with such information, but her own testimonials throw her attempted bifurcation of "third sexes" and "transsexuality" into question.

A particularly glaring oversight is the text's refusal to distinguish between whether hijras lack the *desire* to transition or the *ability*. Despite frequently noting their impoverishment, marginalization, and ostracism from wider society, Nanda barely lingers on Indian society's dehumanization and mistreatment of the hijra, opting instead to wax rhapsodic about Hindu scripture, theology, and the supposed "enshrinement" and "veneration" of the hijra that in the final calculus amounts to less than a hunk of bread. That hijras attempt to justify their existence to a Hindu society in Hindu terms should not be seen as remarkable, given that their religious appeals for dignity *do not work.*

Indeed, the text fails at the fundamental level of affording hijras any agency while simultaneously refusing to reckon at any length with their material circumstances. It chases the ghost of "reverence" without once situating the hijra as individuals constantly negotiating with a hostile and eliminationist regime that barely acknowledges their existence and strenuously denies them the means to self-actualize. To Serena Nanda, the hijra are an exotic prop, a key to the puzzle of undermining European gender norms without resorting to the 'barbarity' of transsexualist 'medicalization'. Her whitewashing of a non-Western culture's bigotry and brutalization of a demographic is only marginally less bizarre than her confounding distaste and seeming resentment towards transsexuals.

On that note, we ought to touch upon one of the most sinister omissions regarding this book, tucked away in endnotes on page 166. In the fourth numbered endnote there, Nanda suggests a slew of texts critiquing the "cultural construction of transsexualism by the medical and mental health professions". Among them is Raymond (1979)—*The Transsexual Empire.*

The foundational text of anthropological third-sexing of the hijra affirmatively cites the most famous transmisogynist in existence, laundering her bilious, fervent hatred of transsexuals into the annals of the queer academy.

# Part Two: Fool Me Once

## Diversity, Inequity, Exclusion

In *Neither Man Nor Woman*, Nanda extensively discusses the years she spent doing fieldwork, interviewing hijras, translating their testimony (twice) and all in all attesting to a level of attempted rigor that makes her misfires nigh inexcusable. If the reader is left wondering how much she is capable of bungling without such preamble, her book *Gender Diversity* leaves no room for doubt.

*Gender Diversity*'s first edition was published in 2000, after the first and second editions of *Neither Man Nor Woman*. It takes what can best be described as an algorithmic approach to analyzing gender expansivity in various non-Western cultures, reproducing the third-sexing framework applied to the hijra in its initial chapters and applying them in turn to various nations. The text aggregates scholarship on Brazil, the Philippines, Indonesia, Polynesia, Thailand, and more. In every instance, it ponders what the existence of these disparate categories could imply for the limited 'Western' view of gender, living up to anthropology's voyeuristic and orientalist roots.

While there are some attempts to incorporate transmasculinities (what the book refers to as "female genders"), it remains fixated on transfeminized populations, as is the academy's wont. There are broad similarities amongst the demographics it studies, including but not limited to being "born male" while expressing a desire for womanhood and femininity, associations with "male homosexuality" oriented around taking up the penetrable "feminized" role in sex, as well as marginalization, ostracism and stigmatization that results in precarity, being locked out of the formal economy, and high rates of survival sex work. We also, once again, see the text attempt bizarre contortions and invocations of cultural relativism, theology, and 'reverence' in order to cast self-evidently abjectified identities as 'institutional genders' in some way, despite the systemic, societal pressures to exclude and expel them.

The fundamental failure plaguing both *Gender Diversity* and Nanda's work on the hijra is the same: a refusal to apply a materialist, empirical, and *feminist* lens to obvious cases of gendered oppression. Nanda appears desperate to romanticize and idealize these exotic, foreign peoples and their enlightened, post-gendered ways, steadfastly ignoring how they exist within extant patriarchies without having toppled the misogynistic regimes that abhor them. Mere observation ought to have indicated that "third sexes" are perfectly compatible with ideologies of male-supremacy and sexual-reproductive exploitation, but we are regaled with florid paeans to Hindu scripture and non-Western 'wisdom' over honest and rigorous scholarship. These texts do not *discuss* third sexes, but seek to *invent* them, to shape the Western understanding of non-Western transfeminized demographics in particular terms.

As before, Nanda's agenda is clarified when the text finally discusses the 'Western' transsexual, this time in chapter eight of *Gender Diversity*.

> *Transsexuals, then, far from being an example of gender diversity, both reflected and reinforced the dominant Euro-American sex/gender ideology in which one had to choose to be either a man or a* (stereotypical) *woman. [Emphasis mine.]*

Nanda's anti-transsexual inclinations are, frankly, difficult to overstate. While she was shrewd enough to not cite Sister Raymond affirmatively in this text, the core thesis of *Transsexual Empire* nonetheless finds its way into her arguments, accompanied by a bevy of cis scholarship speculating on the motives, intentions, and desires of transsexuals. Her words are shot through with what can only be described as a revulsion towards 'medicalization', deriding the transsexual as the product of psychiatric and medical interventions intent on preserving Euro-American patriarchy. Similar to Raymond, she displays an awareness of the surveillance and hyperscrutiny that transsexuals are subjected to by institutions intent on denying them care, yet still sees it fit to denounce them as an equal party to their own policing and suppression.

Her claims that transsexuality reifies gender norms are thrown into particularly sharp relief when she narrates the following tidbit:

> *The availability of the sex-change operation and the emergence of the*

> "transsexual" helps sustain the dominant Euro-American sex/gender system based on binary opposites (Kessler and McKenna 1978). The new male or female sex status may be supported by the construction of a revised life story and certain legal changes, such as revising one's sex on the birth certificate, though this has been repudiated by some American courts. In 2002, for example, a Kansas state court rejected the claim of a transsexual to inherit her husband's property on the basis that her transsexual status did not meet the Kansas legal requirement that only recognizes marriage between persons of the opposite sex. The court acknowledged that, "While [the defendant though] born male, wants and believes herself to be a woman . . . her female anatomy is all man made . . . and thus as a matter of law, [the defendant] is a male" (quoted in Norgren and Nanda 2006:200).

In other words, Nanda holds fast to her claims of transsexuality 'sustaining' the dominant gender paradigm, even when describing institutional delegitimization and denial of transsexual identity! Observing where the power lies and how transsexuals run the risk of recognition being revoked even when they conform to every stricture imposed upon them is, apparently, beyond the author's ability.

By contrast, the book's subsequent section on "Transgenderism" is much more positive and ultimately clarifying.

> *Transgenderism has its foundation in the ancient tradition of androgyny, a view that has made the* crosscultural data from anthropology— *with its descriptions of the positive value of androgyny in some other cultures—particularly relevant to the transgender community (Bolin 1996b:39; Connor 1993; Feinberg 1996). [Emphasis mine.]*
>
> *Unlike transsexuals,* **transgenderists (transpeople)** *do not consider themselves limited to a choice of one of two genders. Transgenderism includes a wide continuum of options, from individuals who wish to undergo sex reassignment surgery to those who wish to live their lives androgynously.*

> *Transgenderists can be narrowly defined as persons who want to change gender roles* without undergoing sexual reassignment surgery; *they can also be defined as "persons who steer a middle course, living with the physical, social, and psychological traits of both genders."* [Emphasis mine.]
>
> Unlike transsexuals *of the 1970s and 1980s, transgenderists today* challenge and stretch the boundaries of the American binary system of sex/gender oppositions *and renounce the American definition of gender as dependent on a consistency of genitals, body type, identity, role behaviors, and sexual orientation.* [Emphasis mine.]

Plainly, Nanda espouses an ideological opposition to bodily transition, *venerating* supposed cross-cultural traditions of androgyny and "embodying *both* genders". (Her own reification of a dualistic gender paradigm, in a book awash with what she calls "third sexes", is surely clever irony.) Her attitudes towards 'transgenderism' closely mirror the way she speaks about "third-sexes", pedestalizing a pure gender "disruption" untainted by medical technologies.

Of course, there remains a singular, burning question that yet remains unasked due to the author's framing.

Are these non-Western third sexes "refusing medicalization" *by choice?*

Not once does Nanda care to interrogate whether inaccessibility, impoverishment, and stigma play a role in keeping the option of bodily transition out of reach. Not once does she care to simply *ask* whether, given the ability to avail of bodily transition, any of her subjects would do so. Such queries would *disrupt* the carefully-constructed antagonism between transsexuals and third-sexes, proving that this, too, is a false binary propped up by zealots to serve their own ends. In addition to Nanda's own informants, later work by Reddy details how hijra consume birth control pills by the handful in their pursuit of breasts, and A. Revathi's autobiography *The Truth About Me* explicates the connection between hijra identity and trans politics. Across the globe, transfeminized individuals from disparate cultures are united by their shared struggles for legibility, set against hegemonies that seek to dehumanize, delegitimize, and degender us, keeping crucial healthcare and the very means of survival out of our hands.

There is very much worth in juxtaposing the Western transsexual and the hijra, but Serena Nanda is far too transmisogynistic to accord that endeavor its due dignity. She does not seek the emancipation or actualization of any of her subjects, pursuing instead a mythical third-sex that can serve as an avatar for "expanding" the West's gendered possibilities.

How ironic, then, that she set off around the world in search of this third sex, when she could very well have found it right at home.

## Whipping Third-Sexed Individual

In *Whipping Girl*, Julia Serano defines and discusses "third-sexing" as follows:

> *Cissexual people who are in the earliest stages of accepting transsexuality ... will often come to see trans people as inhabiting our own unique gender category that is separate from "woman" and "man." I call this act* third-gendering (or third-sexing). *While some attempts at third-gendering trans people are clearly meant to be derogatory or sensationalistic (such as "she-male" or "heshe") ...*

Serano here touches upon a core aspect of transmisogyny, central not only to the many ways in which we are denigrated and slurred, but also characteristic to how we are often depicted and sexualized in media. Terms like "trap", "futa", "dickgirl", and others regard transsexual women as an exotified amalgam of discrete sexual characteristics while simultaneously refusing to name us as *women*, or even *human*, reducing the transsexual body to an object for consumption. *Whipping Girl* also notes how transsexual women in non-pornographic media are still often either degendered or hypersexualized—sometimes both—routinely employing cissexual male actors in drag to represent a garish, parodic approximation of us, or featuring transsexual sex workers who are accorded no humanity and treated as little better than props, frequent disposed of in simultaneously violent and titillating ways.

We thus serve as objects of macabre fascination for cissexuals, either a hypersexualized fantasy with no autonomy or agency of its own, or a monstrous creature whom it is permissible to abhor, violate, and brutalize. Our transgression of gendered strictures, our demonstration of sex's mutability and unfixity is a capital offense that most react to with an irrational fury. Our existence is itself an abomination to a heterosexual, male-supremacist regime, one that must be stamped out and denied at every turn.

Therefore, we are only ever subconsciously regarded as women. We are *womanized* in the way everything considered beneath a Man is feminized, yet our womanhood is repudiated, even as those who seek to destroy us bring the full force of misogynistic degradation to bear. We are assaulted and told we invited assault, that our *deviancy* and *perversion* and pretensions to womanhood carries implicit permission for deviants and perverts to treat us like women. We are discriminated against in employment and housing, frequently impoverished and turned out onto the streets, pushed disproportionately into survival sex work, and routinely face stringent access barriers to transition technologies.

The Enlightened West, in all its wisdom, already has a Third Sex: the tranny.

# Part Three: After Nanda

## Gender Imperialism

In their paper *Begging for change*, Vaibhav Saria speaks about the Indian Supreme Court's 2014 opinion on the petition filed by National Legal Services Authority, or NALSA, concerning India's transgender and hijra populations. Saria notes that the judgment argues for the hijras' "right" to self-identify as a "third-gender", stating:

> 'Hijras/Eunuchs, therefore, have to be considered as *Third Gender,* over and above binary genders *under our Constitution and the laws' [para. 74] [Emphasis mine]*
> It becomes imperative to first assign them their proper "sex". As TGs

> *in India are* neither male nor female, *treating them as belonging to either of the aforesaid categories, is the denial of these constitutional rights. [para. 119] [Emphasis mine]*

Saria themself observes that:

> *The concept of* tritiya prakriti *(third nature/sexuality/gender) and myths from the Ramayana and the Mahabharata are marshalled as evidences for the hijras' historical presence in South Asia,* while the two ethnographies on hijras by Serena Nanda (1991) and Gayatri Reddy (2005) are cited *to refer to the* religious and political significance of hijras in everyday Hindu lives *and the Mughal royal courts. [Emphasis mine.]*

Here is a morbid, maddening irony: anthropological scholarship, distinctly *Western* anthropological scholarship, that for decades has touted the maxim of 'binary gender' being an 'imposed', 'colonial' concept, has now been cited by an Indian court in an opinion that explicitly third-sexes the hijra and purports that recognizing them as women would 'violate their constitutional rights'. It is seemingly only imperialism when populations who seek the technologies of transition and legible womanhood are granted access to them, while the opinions of Western academics shaping local politics is merely sparkling scholarship.

For it must be stated that Nanda's work is not by any means the sole culprit implicated in the academic third-sexing of non-Western demographics. Rather, it is the basis upon which a corpus of such work rests, spawned by institutional interests that seek self-aggrandizement at the expense of orientalized, exotified, and degendered people. The inexplicable demonization of the transsexual and of transition itself undergirds attitudes that demand transfeminized individuals trap themselves in gender-ambiguous amber, over and above heeding their own desires to reshape their sex.

Reddy, for example—whose ethnography is cited alongside Nanda's—is frequently credited with building upon Nanda's work and rectifying her most egregious flaws. It is a fascinating characterization, given that Reddy herself is exonerative of Nanda's work, limiting her critiques of the ethnography only to the first edition and stating of the second:

> *However—and this is particularly germane to my characterization of changing representations of hijras in the literature—Nanda's own thinking and work on hijras appears to have shifted during the last decade. In the second edition of her ethnography, published in 1999, not only has Nanda omitted the preface by Money, she has also reframed her analysis in line with recent developments in gender theory and anthropological modes of inquiry and representation, paying greater attention to the historicopolitical contexts of current scholarship (Nanda, pers. comm.). Perhaps, in addition to signifying changes in hijras' lives over the course of this past decade, these shifts in analytic frameworks and ideologies of representation are a testimony to changing theoretical winds and modes of ethnographic crafting.*

Given that I have based my prior estimation of Nanda's work very much on the second edition, my concerns remain unallayed.

Reddy, furthermore, is prone to reproducing the worst of Nanda's flaws, as illustrated by the following excerpt:

> *Perhaps more deleterious to their health than this unrestricted use of oral contraceptives is hijras' recent habit of injecting themselves with estrogen and progesterone concentrates, bought illegally from the local pharmacies. Not only were they completely unaware of exactly how these products affected their hormone levels and more generally their bodies, none of them would go to a doctor or nurse either to get a prescription or in order to be injected. Shanti claimed to know how to give an injection, having "watched a doctor many times," and it was to her that hijras under the tank went for their weekly injections. Shanti not only had no training, but she used the same needle for multiple injections, facilitating the transmission of HIV (among other infections).*

*Although hijras had heard that these* golis *and* sudis *(injections) were bad for them, they also knew that these substances produced results. Given their strong desire for a* chati *[breasts], they felt this risk was worth taking. The yearning to possess womanly attributes—breasts being one of the most visible and significant of these—was an extremely important motive for such practices.*

While concerns over needle hygiene are more than warranted (and easily solved by making syringes more readily available), acquiring unprescribed hormonal treatments is far safer and more commonplace than most believe. Most transfeminized people languish under regimes that refuse to prescribe us essential transition care, leading many to rely on alternative sources of treatment and community networks of knowledge. Reddy comes across as ignorant of how difficult it is for most of us to acquire prescriptions, of how common it is for us to be under-dosed and placed on dangerous regimens that effectively induce menopause—*by medical professionals*—or indeed avoid mistreatment from doctors, belying the absence or omission of a transsexual perspective that could have proved clarifying. At the very least, meditating on whether this refusal to meet with medical professionals is based on prior experiences could have proved fruitful.

The very next section after this discussion of hormones is entitled "The Mimesis of Femininity and Parodic Gender Subversion". Reddy's reproduction of Nanda's framing does not end here, as her justification for referring to hijras as "mimetics" is also rooted in gestational capacity, and relies on *the same story that Nanda related!*

> "There was once a hijra named Tarabai who desperately wanted children of her own. So she went to Ajmer Baba and asked for this wish to be granted. Only, she said, "I want a child to be produced in my womb," and did not explicitly ask for it to be born. So her pregnancy continued for several months and finally, unable to bear the pain and burden any longer, Tarabai slit her stomach and removed the baby, killing herself and the baby. But to this day, hijras who go to Ajmer Baba's

*dargah [tomb] inevitably pay homage to Tarabai as well." This story was recounted by hijras as "proof" that they "cannot have children," and by virtue of this fact "are not women" (Nanda 1990). [Note—this is the renounced* first *edition of Nanda's book]*

Like Nanda, Reddy's callous detachment stems from fundamentally viewing the hijra less as an oppressed group whose conditions are a product of a patriarchal society and more as potential *subversives*, whose 'performance' has edifying potential for how others can think about and navigate gendered systems. As she puts it:

*In the case of hijras, for instance, does their gendered performance constitute parodic subversion, or does it merely constitute a resignification of normative gender ideals and practices? Hijras clearly express an overwhelming desire for the accouterments of femininity. Does this imply that hijras are merely reinscribing given, normative patterns of gender ascription and aspiration? Equally clearly in many contexts, hijras appear to perceive their identities as outside the binary frame of gendered reference. Given hijras' realization of the constructed nature of their (gendered) identities, does this in itself constitute their performance as parody and therefore as potentially subversive? What constitutes resistance in such a scenario? In other words, are hijras primary agents of gender subversion in the Indian cultural context, or are they uncritically reinscribing gendered categories through their desires and practice? [Emphasis mine.]*

The hijras' material conditions, positionality under a heterosexual regime, or even their activism and resistance to their society's stigmatization come second to the navel-gazing solipsism of cissexual academics, rendering judgment from on high. It is a thoroughly hegemonic gaze, a fetishistic view in the original sense of the term, where the hijras' symbolic value as either "gender-insurgents" or "upholders of patriarchy" matters more than their literal humanity, dignity, and survival. This parasitic, extractive impulse towards a marginalized population is frankly sickening, to say nothing of the sheer temerity required to postulate that people who are so thoroughly rejected and repressed by their society might be active agents in reinforcing the very institutions depriving and dehumanizing them—a conclusion only an academic could dream up.

The 2014 NALSA opinion that cited Reddy was not legislation, as such, but was to form the basis of a draft bill. Saria goes on to discuss how the opinion did not consult India's transgender or hijra communities, nor did further legislation based on it. A series of legal missteps culminated in a ghastly 2016 bill, named 'The Transgender Persons (Protection of Rights) Bill of 2016', which dramatically expanded the state's role in gender recognition, requiring all trans people to first obtain a 'Transgender Certificate' and submit themselves to institutional scrutiny as a precursor to legal recognition. This proposition tore up all previous discussions on the right to self-identification, resulting in the mobilization of Indian trans communities in protest of a bill that was putatively meant to secure their rights. From Raymond to Nanda to Reddy to NALSA, we can trace a path from Western transmisogynistic fundamentalism to the legal, institutionalized Third-Sexing of all Indian trans people.

*That* is the legacy of Western academia, of cultural anthropology, of a field playing at decolonialism proving to be an instrumental imperialist accomplice to India's codification of degendering.

## The Truth About Me

*The Truth About Me: A Hijra Life Story* is an autobiographical novel by A. Revathi, translated into English from Tamil. It is a blunt, harsh, and oftentimes difficult account of the life of a hijra, a population so thoroughly marginalized that such firsthand accounts are a remarkable rarity. Revathi discusses her childhood as a feminine 'boy', her lifelong identification with girlhood and womanhood, and the arduous journey she had to undergo in order to live authentically. She is candid about various aspects of her community and their way of life, and attests to the pursuit of surgical and hormonal treatments by hijra, so that their embodiment may match their identity.

In other words, she conclusively describes the ways in which hijra experiences parallel so-called "Western" transsexuality.

Her own words on the subject, excerpted from a speech she delivered at a Koovagam festival, express it best:

> ... *The feelings I have are natural and they should be recognized as such. We want those like us, born as men, but with feminine feelings to have the right to sex-change surgery. All I ask is that you accept as worthy of respect what you've all along considered unnatural and illegal.* ... If there is something wrong with a woman's uterus, you don't hesitate to surgically remove it. If you happen to know that your child-to-be is a girl, you don't mind destroying the foetus. Thus, each one of your acts falls foul of the law, of nature. But you bring up issues of nature and law only where certain things are concerned. Listen, I am not diseased. I consider myself a woman. But I possessed the form of a man. I wanted to rid myself of that form and live as a complete woman. How can that be wrong? [Emphasis mine.]
>
> In some countries, government-run hospitals counsel people like me, put us on a course of hormones, carry out sex reassignment surgery and acknowledge our right to change our sex. Such women go to work, get married, do as other women do. We want the Indian state to do the same: provide us with counseling, put us on a course of hormones and assist with sex-change surgeries. *Since law and society in this country do not acknowledge our right to live as we wish, we are forced to beg, take up sex work, and suffer as a consequence.* Today, sex-change operations are carried out in a few private clinics, where surgical procedures are seldom followed, and which do not extend the sort of care we require afterwards. Many of us end up suffering all sorts of infections. We want to live as women, and if we are granted the facilities that will enable us to do so, we'll live as other women do. *We were not born to beg or do sex work.* [Emphasis mine.]

My nation, my society, my state, and its blighted culture, rarely allow women like Revathi to speak.

Heed her words, and heed them well.

## A Too-Short History of Transmisogyny

*A Short History of Transmisogyny*, authored by Jules Gill-Peterson, aspires to a cross-cultural, historical reckoning with global regimes of transmisogyny.

Gill-Peterson's work is fiery and insightful, lucid on the topic of transsexuality and its stigmatization. Her book's introduction firmly situates the struggles of trans women alongside the hijra, travesti, street queens, Two-Spirits, and others, attempting to articulate a unified politics of resistance against the worldwide suppression of transfemininity. I eagerly anticipated this book's release earlier this year, both due to my familiarity with her scholarship and because I had high hopes that, as a desi transsexual woman, Gill-Peterson would do the topic justice.

I am grateful to her for the stark reminder that identity is not the sole determiner of outlook.

> To understand what happened in the wake of Bhoorah's murder, it's important to say that hijras were not then—and are not today—transgender. Even though the story of the global trans panic weaves through their experience, it doesn't mean they should be interpreted as trans women. *Hijras, for one thing, are arguably* much older than the Western concept of gender *through which trans emerged as boundary crossing.* [Emphasis mine.]

This is, ultimately, an argument with its roots in academic decolonial feminism, a school that considers the "rigid gender binary" to be a colonial export. Much ink has been spilled condemning colonial regimes for their corruption of precolonial, prelapsarian non-Western cultures, whose 'expansive gender-systems' allowed for populations like the hijra to 'flourish'. It is a familiar song and dance, though a wearying one by now, if you've been paying attention.

In an interview for *The Cut*, Gill-Peterson makes her views on this explicit:

> *"There are many people who don't necessarily share this Euro-American definition of "trans woman": two-spirit people in the United States, hijras in British colonial India, travestis in Argentina."*

And so the band plays on.

It is difficult to know where to begin when contesting such a naive, idealistic view of precolonial societies, precisely *because* it is so trivially contradicted by the most perfunctory empirical observations. Hindu scripture, predating the very concept of a "West" by millennia, codifies the inferiority of women and the necessity for wives to subordinate themselves to husbands. Even during colonial times, the outlawing of widow burning was a pitched battle between Indian activists and the upper-caste Hindu elites. (The edict was eventually reverted to appease that selfsame elite.) I do not know how to explain to learned academics that sexual objectification and reproductive exploitation were not innovations that the West pioneered, nor do I know how to explain that a historical record of "asceticism", of hijra being prescribed a livelihood of begging for alms at ceremonies, is not "reverence" or an "institutionalized gender-role", but marginalization.

Bubbles Khanum, a member of the Pakistani khwaja sira community, has this to say on the topic:

> *Sir Syed Ahmed Khan, commonly known as a hero for reforming education for the Indians, wrote a letter to the British demanding an action being taken against the Hijra community. Our lives before all that are often glorified excessively in attempts to convince the modern transphobic society that we belong here but the truth is, patriarchy has existed for thousands of years, where women have been subjugated, the Hijras were no exception and were not seen as equals. They were still victims of gendered violence, were ostracized to live in their own communes, had to heavily rely on religiosity and spirituality to get*

> whatever respect they did, and at most all those efforts managed to get some of them secondary roles in the society such as advisors or harem guards. Moving forward the over glorification of the past does more harm than good as that is not what we want to go back to just to undo the damage the colonizers have done.

I wish to reiterate her message, grim though it may be: There is no salvation awaiting us in a glorified past that does not exist. If we are to advocate for our humanity, our legibility, and our liberty, it will be as a part of something new, something unprecedented, something we do not as yet have names for. You do not want the 'veneration' that the holy men of my culture reserve for us.

Oh, save my sisters from the "reverence" of this cursed land and its misbegotten people.

# Part Four: A Tale of Two Genders

## It's the Power Differential, Stupid

Ostensibly, cultural anthropology's gender odyssey is motivated by a desire to undermine and denaturalize the dualist, dichotomous nature of the Western gender system. Nanda's elevation of "transgenderism" over "transsexuality" invokes a rosy view of anthropology's role in unearthing a rich cross-cultural history of androgynous traditions, while Reddy's meditation on "gender performance" seeks to gauge the subversive potential of hijra existence. These are, at least nominally, *feminist* goals, which make the neglect of feminist frameworks in their pursuit all the more confounding.

For the idea that a "Third Sex" could shake the very foundations of patriarchy is not merely misguided, it is unfathomably naive. While "the gender binary" is a good shorthand for summarizing many aspects of the heterosexual regime—namely the division of humanity into exhaustively two naturalized non-overlapping sexes—it does not convey the most important characteristic.

Succinctly, mere categorization does not constitute violence and injustice.

Rather, the *aggrandizement of one category at the expense of the other(s)*, enforced and upheld at the socio-cultural and institutional level, is what makes "the gender binary" unjust.

In even plainer terms: "It's male-supremacy, stupid."

The existence of a third sex does no more to challenge societal male-supremacy than does the existence of a fourth, fifth, or even *second* sex. Every sex that is not the First Amongst Sexes, that is not the Most Vaunted, Most Esteemed, and Most Adored Sex, simply becomes another sexual resource to be exploited. Patriarchy's basis is not inherently a *dichotomy*, and the "rich history" of transfeminized populations across cultures—*including the West*—ought to have illustrated that plainly. The existence of hijras did little to challenge Hinduism's enshrinement of male-supremacy, and the existence of transsexuals has only made the West's ideological commitments to a dualistic sex model more pronounced.

Thus Third-Sexing, far from being a *challenge* to patriarchy, seems to be a surprisingly historical feature of its operation.

Systems of repression, ultimately, do not revise their most cherished imperatives based on democratic feedback. What they cannot extinguish entirely, they repurpose or recuperate.

In many ways, Nanda's work *did* have the potential to rectify various failures of the second wave and push further our understanding of the social construction of sex. Had she not been ideologically committed to seeing the hijra as male ascetics, had she looked at Hinduism's repressive edicts with a feminist instead of an orientalist eye, and if she had been willing to connect the plight of the hijra to that of the transsexual and even cissexual woman, all rendered sexual resources under regimes of heterosexuality, we might have arrived at transmisogyny theory decades early.

Instead, we have the romanticization of a faith under whose auspices a nationalistic, theocratic government is today fomenting religious fascism and attempting to eradicate the hijra way of life entirely.

Hindus, it would appear, have little reverence for the hijra after all.

## Towards a Feminist Understanding of Third-Sexing

Cultural anthropology may have coined and codified "third-sexing" to legitimize the degendering of transfeminized populations in the Third World, but that does not mean that the term is inherently without value, or is not an observation of a real phenomenon. After all, the treatment of the hijra as something outside of gendered duality, as "possessing the qualities of both", as well as misconceptions of hijras all being born "hermaphroditic" or intersex, are rooted in Indian and Hindu culture.

Indeed, in the eyes of Indian patriarchy, "hijra" *is* an expansive category, one that is meant to encompass all those deemed—bluntly—sexually 'defective'. Girls who do not menstruate may be considered hijra, and while intersex individuals were the minority amongst them, they too are stigmatized and ostracized into hijra communities. The "third sex", such as it is, is not a prescriptive category, but a dumping-ground, a landfill in which to deposit everyone that a society organized around the reproductive imperative considers extraneous and aberrant.

Such an attitude is predictive of prevailing attitudes towards homosexuality, a subject on which India's track record is indeed abysmal. It must be recalled that historically in the West and in many cultures even today, homosexuality was first and foremost conceptualized as *gendered deviance*, rather than as an aspect of one's identity independent of sex. Bizarre myths of lesbians as androgenized "tribades" with massive, penetrating clitorises existed alongside a corrective, curative fixation on "male effeminacy", because patriarchal regimes do not care for the reality or the granularity of an expansive queer existence.

Simply put, under patriarchy, *heterosexuality is the only legitimate mode of existence, and all deviations from it are similarly punished.*

Nor is this contempt for all those who contravene the reproductive imperative limited to queer individuals. In India, infertile women—or even women who bear their husbands only daughters and no sons—face mistreatment, violence, treatment as "untouchable", and expulsion from their families, as do widows. Womanhood being synonymized with gestation means that it comes with an *expiration date*, past which a woman who either could not perform the one function that accorded her any worth, or cannot do so anymore, becomes yet more offal to discard and sweep out onto the streets. Dworkin, in her essay *The Coming Gynocide*, observes a similar phenomenon in the West, where underfunded and overflowing care homes are disproportionately comprised of old *women*, as is the composition of elderly individuals on state or medical assistance.

> *"Old women do not have babies; they have outlived their husbands; there is no reason to value them. They live in poverty because the society that has no use for them has sentenced them to death."*

If you are not of the First Sex, pride and heir to your line, Third-Sexing will come for you sooner or later.

None of this is to attempt to collapse all forms of gendered oppression into a singular category, to erase distinction and equivocate between related yet distinct forms of patriarchal violence. Nor do I believe it is edifying or productive to try to determine whether a woman forced to bear children for a family that reviles her, or a woman expelled from society and forced to live on the margins, suffers more.

Rather, this is an explication of the underlying *root* of patriarchy, its core mechanisms and systems that constitute the guiding principles of (trans)misogyny, lesbophobia—*all* instances of gender-marginalization. Sex is not quite as *binary* as advertised, because the heterosexual regime has always regarded people as one of *human, broodmare,* or *freak*. If you are not a person with autonomy, then you are a vessel for those who are ... and if you cannot even be *that*, then you are a waste of flesh, something to be *fucked, killed,* or *both*.

The butch derided and beaten as a delusional "he-she", the tranny who can be endlessly violated, and even the woman who merely refuses to have children, are bound by this commonality. If we cannot participate in reproduction, we must be *fixed* ... or disposed of.

## Subversivism and Transition

A disturbing and recurring theme in the literature regarding both supposed third-sexes and "Western" transsexuality is the positioning of transsexuality as an inherently less subversive, more regressive, and unquestionably *patriarchal* practice. Oftentimes, the justifications for these audacious claims refer to "medicalization" in terms no less stigmatizing and fearmongering than Raymond herself, or the modern Gender-Conservative movement that echoes her. Nanda makes this core to the distinction between the "transgenderist" and the "transsexual", elevating the former at the expense of the latter, a view grounded entirely in considering bodily transition an artificial and fundamentally assimilationist process.

If we are to humor this viewpoint at all, we are forced to admit that such a conception of transsexuality does not survive any length of empirical scrutiny. Not only have transsexuals been historically *barred* and *gatekept* from transition care, forced to play dress-up and memorize cribbed responses for doctors who would arbitrarily and gleefully revoke their rights to the care they desperately needed, our identities have time and time again been subject to challenge, denial, and contestation by others. Nor can a population so thoroughly stigmatized, impoverished, and routinely subject to patriarchal violence "uphold" the very system stripping them of humanity and personhood.

This categorization of transition and revulsion towards those who avail of it seems particularly distasteful and irresponsible in today's climate, with a global reactionary moral panic scapegoating and vilifying transsexuals and seeking to criminalize all transition technologies. Morbidly, many justifications for outlawing transsexuality rely upon these decades-old tropes and popularized notions of "untested", "mutilating", "medicalizing" processes that will never be accorded legitimacy no matter how many positive outcomes are cited.

Even the widely-discredited Cass Review, a document that is being used to justify outlawing transition care despite its glaring methodological shortcomings, gallingly invokes the constructed opposition of transsexuality with "true" gender nonconformity on page *fourteen*.

> Secondly, medication is binary, *but the fastest growing group identifying under the trans umbrella is non-binary, and we know even less about the outcomes for this group. Some of you* will also become more fluid in your gender identity *as you grow older.* [Emphasis mine.]

It is a testament to the utter depravity and cataclysmic negligence of solipsistic academic literature that deeply entrenched conservative attitudes towards bodily transition, attitudes that make life harder for marginalized transsexuals at the institutional level, have for so long been repackaged and propped up as some manner of far-sighted feminist ethos. In reality, transsexuals are routinely denied *bodily autonomy* and the *right to our own sex*, systemically prevented from accessing the care that would allow us to take our sex into our own hands due to cissexist anxieties around 'fertility' or reproductive capacity. The modern anti-transsexual moral panic stems from a conception of reproductive viability being the prime determiner of individual worth, over and above individuals' own wishes, regarding every transitioned person as a societal failure and a "lifelong medical patient". It underwrites the notion that parents who abuse queer and trans children have more of a right to their children's bodies than queer and trans children have to their own, and relies upon thoroughly eugenical logics in order to devalue and dehumanize all those who pursue bodily transition.

In the final calculus, how "subversive" bodily transition is should not matter to anyone more than the fact that transition care is an absolute necessity for many, many people, but the pretense that transition is in any way "normative" or "regressive" under patriarchal regimes hell-bent on eradicating it—morally mandating it out of existence, one might say—is facile, absurd, and an exercise in idealist sophistry. The normalization and elevation of this idea is not merely abhorrent, but actively eliminationist.

## Hermeneutical Injustice and External Observers

In *Neither Man Nor Woman*, Nanda engages in a particularly damaging rhetorical sleight of hand. The book is careful to declare its reliance on testimonials, to stress its reproduction of meticulously translated firsthand accounts, and to overall give the impression that Nanda's conclusions are based upon an impartial and neutral observation of the facts and details presented to her. As we saw several times earlier, this is a farce, given how the author selectively emphasizes some details while minimizing others, presents the information through a thoroughly ideological lens, and at times fails to even realize the significance of some of her observations. Nor are the mistakes and misrepresentations covered so far in this essay by any means exhaustive, and Nanda's inability to connect the hijra engaging in both Hindu and Muslim practices to India's caste system and islamophobia, or her surprising credulity when narrating a "myth" that "permits all hijra to travel on trains for free", could be the subjects of essays just as long.

Her ethnography acutely demonstrates the hollowness of academic 'objectivity', revealing it to be nothing but an additional facet of the epistemic violence marginalized populations are confronted with. When Serena Nanda is allowed to set the discursive tone of hijra understanding in the West—and apparently in Indian Supreme Court opinions, too—the inclusion of testimonials is so much theater, gesturing towards the participation of marginalized demographics while maintaining a strictly hegemonic outlook. It reflects exactly how Indian society already treats the hijras: denying their every attempt to claim womanhood and insisting on third-sexing and stigmatizing them, while relying heavily on damnable religious rationalizations that are already routinely invoked to sanctify so much patriarchal violence.

I do not pretend to be able to definitively claim that every single hijra thinks of herself as a woman. However, when hijras engage in activism to advocate for legal recognition as women, when they participate in *Aurat* Marches (*aurat* means *woman*) holding signs that say "Hijras Are Women" and "Trans Women Are Women. SHUT UP", it is safe to state that presenting hijra identity as mystical, complex, and utterly beyond any affinity to "Western" transsexuality is deliberate silencing and a baldfaced attempt to further the hermeneutical injustice desi cultures already subject them to.

Most reprehensible, however, are the attempts to paint any desires for solidarity between hijras and transsexuals as "Western imperialism", or to enshrine their degendering as a valiant "decolonial" effort to preserve non-Western cultures in all their bloodstained glory. As a disowned daughter of this culture, I wish to state in no uncertain terms:

*If a culture's preservation depends on the violation and degendering of and denial of dignity to my sisters, then it should join every other extant regime that thrives on injustice, upon the ash-heap.*

(Trans)misogyny is not a cultural value worth preserving. The development of a cross-cultural transsexual and transfeminist consciousness, rooted in the recognition of how our identities and struggles are similarly shaped, is not imperialism. It is a struggle for liberation, one that queer academia is heinously eager to oppose, and one whose proponents shall no longer be spoken over.

## Conclusion: Voices of the Damned

I am not, by any means, a perfect representative of all hijra, all desi trans women, or even of all desi transfeminists.

*Hijra*, I am told, and as some of the above scholarship notes, is less an identity and more a community. Most, if not all hijras are transfeminized, but not all who are transfeminized desi individuals are hijra. Indeed, as Saria notes, the emergent trans identity in India has a certain class character to it, with many affluent trans women seeking to distance themselves from the abjectified hijra and advocate for themselves as a more respectable breed of queer.

Their treasonous politics will not soon be forgiven.

Personally, I am very much a transsexual desi dyke, a distinction I draw not as disavowal, but out of respect. I have no house, no kin, and do not have the honor of calling any hijra my family. I suffered the closet alone, quietly, biding my time until I could make good my escape. I am not as brave as most hijra, and I am significantly more privileged, able to leverage material advantages most of them will never have access to. I speak in the tongue of our colonizers, a bloodsoaked gift that can by itself determine our ability to cross the borders that confine us. I avoided a fate, a prison with saffron bars, that so many of my sisters will never have the opportunity to. This is a knowledge—a certainty—that sears at my soul in ways I don't have names for.

Do you understand?

Sometimes, more often than I'd like to admit, *I* don't understand. I don't understand how I can live with myself.

Knowing this ... attempting to comprehend the scale of it, the enormity, the sheer totality of the torture my society puts women like me through ... do you understand what it feels like to encounter queer dogma in the West that touts the hijra as a "recognized Third Gender"?

How can I express to you how hysteria-inducing it is to see the hijra described as *revered*, when I grew up immersed in the toxic miasma of that 'reverence'?

I am not, by any means, someone with an extensive background on this subject. I am simply a trans woman from the nation in question, who speaks this language, who was exposed to this scholarship, and who, first and foremost, *cares*.

Because so many of my own countrymen, whether cis or trans, whether aligning perfectly with my politics or opposed on every count, simply *do not care*.

All I really did was read shoddy, orientalizing texts that mystify and mangle what it's like to exist under the crushing heel of Third World patriarchy, and I called bullshit.

This is a point I desperately wish to drive home, because I must ask ... why me?

Why did *I* have to make the connection between Sister Raymond's Troon-madness Bible and an anthropological text that launders its ravings into the queer academy's canon?

Why did *I* have to be the one to point out that texts that describe gender-marginalized people as "exaggerated, garish parodies of femininity" was perhaps not an ideal vector for understanding their plight?

I ask because it seems improbable, bordering on impossible, that a book that treats its subjects with such open scorn and derision could go over three decades without its blatant, inhumane cruelty being remarked upon, and yet that seems to be the case.

Then again, it's not like the derision of trans women is new to the hallowed halls of the academy.

Perhaps this is ultimately why the learned ones see us as nothing but costumed natives, putting on a show for their amusement. They are a pantomime, a parade of pretenders in drag, trying to pass off solipsistic, bigoted drivel as an intellectual pursuit, seeing their own artificiality reflected in all they behold. Peel back the curtain, and witness how quickly the mask slips, how the masturbatory indulgences give way to corrosive, hateful screeds.

I ask, but I already know the answer.

And I am not interested in their answers anymore.

No, the charlatans with far too much ink to spill have said enough. Now is the time for the transsexual, the third-sexed woman, the third-world lesbian, and all those who have been reduced to rhetorical props to speak, to *scream*, to ROAR, to raise their voices in a cacophony. Now is the time for the damned to have their due, for the wails of the forgotten to echo above the "civil", silencing din. Now is the time for all those whose struggles have been erased, co-opted, recuperated, disrupted, and sanctified to make themselves known.

Now we will speak, and you will, for the first time, **LISTEN**.

# Conclusion: The Question Has an Answer

## The Day Transphobia Ended

If you're unfamiliar with who Graham Linehan is, he is most famous for being divorced and writing a lot of transphobic tweets. He identifies affirmatively with the gender-conservative movement that has with no sense of irony dubbed itself 'Gender Critical', and thus fosters an online presence that is uncomfortably fixated on trans issues and trans women. On one fateful day, a lone, brave voice posed a question to Linehan, prompting an exchange that I cannot do justice to, but will do my best to paraphrase here.

In response to his utter befuddlement at the idea that "There is no definition of woman", Linehan was asked: "Graham, could you define 'chair' for us real quick?"

Not one to shrink from such a trivial intellectual challenge—no matter how loudly telegraphed the rhetorical trap was—Linehan met this inquiry with the solid rejoinder: "A separate seat for one person, typically with a back and four legs."

"Happy to help but try Google next time. The definition of 'woman' is there, too," he added, no doubt with a hearty chuckle at his own brilliance.

He had no idea what a storm his words would unleash.

With the tripwire triggered, the replies to his foolish rhetorical volley came in fast and furious, pelting him with counterexample after exception after erroneous inclusion. Images of chairs with no legs, bathtubs with four, and all manner of absurd objects were conjured in response to his foolish attempt at an encapsulation of "chair-ness". The killing blow came in the form of a harbinger, a vehicle for Linehan's own personal linguistic apocalypse.

"Chair" the tweet simply stated, suspended above the photographic depiction of a humble, four-legged, one-backed horse.

As the farrier drives shoe into hoof, so too did this tweet hammer home the final nail in the coffin of Gender-Conservative ideology. Having been shown how erroneous, how insufficient, how baldfacedly *absurd* their patterns of thinking were, transphobes had no choice but to capitulate utterly to a Total Transgender Victory. Every transphobic politician resigned in disgrace, while every newspaper that had ever dared to entertain transphobic notions—which is to say, every newspaper—issued a full retraction and announced Judith Butler's coronation as World Monarch. The gender-conservative movement was driven underground, left to languish, huddled around garbage fires made of discarded children's literature, clinging to an image of an imperfect world that had long passed them by.

If only their names had not been lost to time and ill-advised rebranding, we may have been able to honor these valiant heroes, these courageous soldiers who through their collective efforts won the Second Sex Wars.

## Right! ... Right?

Or, you know, *none of that.*

Instead, the transphobic reactionary wave core to the modern Gender-Conservative antifeminist movement only grew more emboldened, accruing more and more funding, institutional legitimacy, and coverage. The relentless push to implement transphobic legislation, from bathroom discrimination to outright bans on transition care, eventually gathered enough momentum and ideological backing to finally pass in various Western jurisdictions. Junk studies, bunk science, and fraudulent reports proliferated, polluting the scientific consensus on trans healthcare, and many politicians either took up the cause of scapegoating a tiny slice of the population for their policy shortcomings, or considered it expedient to abandon us entirely.

How did the champions of trans people and trans rights react to this resurgence of reactionary gender politics and intensifying attacks on queer existence? Largely by posting doctored images of Donald Trump and Elon Musk in a gay relationship, or in dresses, because no crime a man commits can ever compare to a presumed lack of masculinity.

Truly, we are in good hands.

A simple look around at the current state of affairs should clue in even the most tuned-out of us to the blindingly obvious: liberal feminism is fucking dead. It failed to protect abortion rights, it failed to meaningfully issue a challenge to patriarchal rape culture, and absolutely fucking failed every single trans person.

This is not a eulogy. It is not fanfare at witnessing the doddering, shambling corpse of this ideological dead-end finally collapse. It is an autopsy, an accounting, and first and foremost a reckoning with a feminist project that sought to liberate women while refusing to take into account the male-supremacy endemic to patriarchy. The mainstream feminist discourse did not meaningfully challenge the prevailing essentialist model of naturalized sex, nor did it effectively advocate for the bodily autonomy of the gender-marginalized. It is poised to squander even more of the second wave's gains if someone doesn't just. Call. *Bullshit*.

I come not to praise Steinem, but to bury her, and some of her worst accomplices with the bier.

## Listen Up, Liberal

Liberalism is the erroneous belief that one can paper over systemic inequality with enough contract law, consent fetishism, and lip service to 'individual freedom'. It is ruling-class propaganda that bamboozles people into thinking that token mass participation in the political process can outweigh the hoarding of wealth and privileges and control over the means of cultural production.

When applied to feminist thought, this ideological defect reframes the imbalances of power in the sexual economy to a simple matter of 'restricted freedoms' that can, one by one, be alleviated legislatively through state protectionism. If women are underpaid, then we shall simply make it illegal to pay them less, in much the same way one would apply a bandage to a gaping wound. Surely treating symptoms without investigating causes would eventually solve the problem. We need not inquire why women are paid less, what factors are contributing to their labor being undervalued, and whether there are underlying causes leading to such treatment that legislation alone cannot remedy.

It is, in a sentence, a Human Resources approach to managing rape culture.

What liberal ideologies are worst at addressing, of course, are questions pertaining to their own violences, the injustices and disparities they promulgate, perpetuate, and thrive on, just underneath the facade of bringing all parties to the same table. They have never been able to confront the truth of how workers are far less free to negotiate terms than bosses, concerned more with the image of happy coordination than the reality of who has signed the dotted line with a gun to her head.

For feminism, this became a maxim of *choice*, a true punchline to the joke that is gender. Women can choose to be empowered, careerist, liberated, and professional, or we can 'choose' to be domestically confined, saddled with the bulk of reproductive labor, and have little recourse to violations of our body, dignity, and personhood. With the benefit of hindsight, it is plain to see how this strain of 'feminism' was never a serious counterpoint to patriarchal relations.

Fundamentally, the liberal-feminist model is motivated by a desire to ignore the elephant, even as it tramples the room's occupants underfoot. It adopts a language of ersatz gender equality, presuming that so long as barriers to individual freedom are addressed, everyone can benefit from the system equally. In matters of coercion, violence, non-economic interests, or even the simple identification of cultural factors contributing to these issues, this approach falls short entirely. Questions of subjugation, violence, and suppression are ignored in favor of trust in institutions and the singular guiding principle: "But what if the oppressed party consents?"

It was PR.

Missing from any of this is an analysis of the mechanisms of patriarchy, the heterosexuality at the heart of it all. There is a pervasive incuriosity permeating the school of thought, a wilful omission of the exploitation, extractivism, and sheer sexual sadism that underlies a misogynistic society.

The dirty secret is that liberal feminism, for all its paeans to gender parity, did not ever meaningfully contradict the naturalization of sex, the idea that on some essential level, women are simply synonymous with gestation, with child-rearing, with *less*. It was content to simply proffer the platitude that *if* a woman wishes to exceed her station, then she should surely be *allowed* to. How much could women's liberation cost, girls? Ten dollars?

This was never an attitude, a rigorous school of thought, or an approach that could radically challenge the retrenchment of Gender-Conservatism. When the gains of feminist victories and economic independence started to pile up, the patriarchal recuperation and reactionary backlash was focused and swift. Right-wing attitudes found many masks to conceal misogynistic intent, sometimes wearing an anti-capitalist hat to talk about the meaningless grind of women's workplaces, and at other times adopting feminist theatrics to conflate "women's rights" with genital inspections.

Crucially, when Gender-Conservatism asked on what basis we should consider trans women to be *real*, *authentic* women, liberal feminism simply shrugged and began babbling about category errors, as though philosophical technicalities are an adequate substitute for advocacy. They are women because they *choose* to be, and who are we to deny them that *choice*?

As far as endorsements go, this one rings hollow. The gender anxieties underpinning trans people's mutable sex, the ability to "cross" heterosexuality's impermeable barrier, won out over a half-hearted attempt to frame the question of our rights as *free expression* rather than a struggle against patriarchy's attempts to deny us bodily autonomy and eradicate us.

We were, to speak it plain, abandoned. Women, queers, and trannies alike.

I guess we *chose* wrong.

CONCLUSION: THE QUESTION HAS AN ANSWER

# Round Two

For all its faults, though, wasn't liberal feminism *better*? Wasn't it a kinder, gentler alternative to the second wave that preceded it? The radical feminist movement was categorized by a militant commitment to academic, middle-class white womanhood, championed by the misandry of affluent lesbians, resulting in a stiflingly uniform classist, racist, and transmisogynistic politic. Surely, what followed learned from its mistakes, built upon its strengths, and gave a voice to those whom feminism had historically silenced?

No.

No, not really.

There is a tendency to narrativize history, to draw boundaries and delineations that are far cleaner on paper than they ever were on the ground. It would be as inaccurate to attribute an artificial homogeneity to the second-wave as it would be to assert that liberal feminism successfully addressed its myriad failings. This contextual collapse results partly from a refusal to take feminism seriously as a school of thought, one rife with its own orthodoxies, contradictions, dissidents, theoretical innovations and internal critiques. Feminism has always been fractious, always an arena rather than a solidified platform, with competing and collaborating branches that unify and schism in equal measure.

It is, in short, a *discipline*, and a perpetually evolving one at that.

Attempts to partition the history of feminism into easily-separable waves tend to be just as arbitrary and constructed as patriarchal gender. Audre Lorde and Leslie Feinberg are frequently claimed by "Third Wave" feminism, a categorization that flies in the face of Lorde's two decades of friendship with Adrienne Rich, or Feinberg's gratitude for Rich's support in the acknowledgements of *Transgender Warriors*. Reading their work alone should be sufficient to see where they were inspired by the radical lesbian feminist tradition as well as where they deviated—at least, if one were given to treat feminist subschools with a greater degree of complexity and nuance than trying to label them 'Good' or 'Bad'.

Nor is it anything more than naive ignorance to presume that radical feminism's issues with transmisogyny were what inspired the backlash against it. The reverence accorded to Serena Nanda's corpus of work alone should disabuse that notion, but one need only glance at bell hooks' essay on *Paris Is Burning*, or Judith Butler's commentary on the same, to see that the pathologization of transfemininity, together with the marginalization of transfeminine perspectives, would continue unabated into the era of "kinder, gentler, *inclusive*" feminism.

Just as there is still white feminism following the publication of Crenshaw's paper on intersectionality, transmisogynistic feminism remains alive and well in the years since Sandy Stone's 'postranssexual' manifesto. We still grapple with many of the same prejudices, structures, and institutional biases today that the feminists of the second wave did in their day, and part of the liberal-feminist mythology depends on the ahistorical narrativization denying that stark reality.

If we are to reckon with the failures of feminisms past and present, we have to be *honest* about where those failures lie rather than just patting ourselves on the back for being "so much more enlightened nowadays". We must ask ourselves why a materialist movement allowed itself to be polluted by idealist, essentialist thought, why putative social-constructivists found themselves associating amicably with theologically-inspired fundamentalists like Raymond and Daly. We must also admit that when it came to condemning the TERFs, modern feminists took far greater issue with the 'RF' than they did the 'TE'.

Simply put: Radical feminism saw the most definitive real-world proof of its own theories in the transsexual, and sought to destroy her instead of embracing her.

When perusing these texts, I am assailed, over and over, by the sheer irony of the radical feminist tradition sabotaging itself by vehemently rejecting the conclusions of its own theories. Womanhood is a social positionality constructed through misogynistic violence and sexual-reproductive exploitation, and no case confirms this more than the transsexual woman, whose 'male anatomy' does not spare her in the slightest. Every transsexual woman is the wretched, spurned daughter of the radical feminist thesis, the unwanted validation of its most fundamental tenets that it sought to terminate.

For all their insight, clarity of purpose, rhetorical verve, and righteous conviction, when push came to shove, the radical feminists proved no better than the gender-essentialists they once sought to condemn. They felt greater sorority with the rambling lunatics babbling about 'sexed souls' than the women whose very existence was so unconscionable to patriarchal regimes that we are to this day faced with utter annihilation.

In these texts, I found the language to describe my own making and unmaking. From their words, I forged the fury of my own purpose. They were, in their own day, at their best, brilliant and brave women.

And they still abandoned their own ideals out of sheer disgust.

Look upon our faces, and see the truth none of you were able to bear.

The Radical Feminists are no more, not in any sense worthy of the name, not in any form that honors their original principles. Do not consider this a tragedy, however, especially when the conclusive chapters are yet to be written.

After all, it always falls upon disowned daughters to clean up their foremothers' messes.

## The Measure of a Misandrist

This is, ultimately, where most critiques of radical feminism go wrong, even when supposedly made with trans women's vilification in mind. It is a too-popular idea that radical feminism was too harsh, too critical and too antagonistic towards *men*. After all—goes the reasoning—is not the fixation on trans women, the denial of our womanhood, and the maligning of us as ontologically predatory a consequence of their gender-absolutism? Is not resorting to 'misandry' in response to society's misogyny also wrong?

Such arguments fail to be compelling for two reasons, the first of which *should* be obvious: transmisogyny *is not misandry*. The transmisogynist does not treat trans women the way she treats men, even if she refers to a trans woman as a man in the process of degendering her. Even if a transmisogynist bears an authentic antipathy for men, there is a crucial difference in how she regards trans women: namely, as an *acceptable target of misogynistic degradation*. Trans women's bodies are dissected and scrutinized, our behavior pathologized and sexualized, and our own testimony discarded as unreliable, insubstantial, and immaterial. We are dehumanized, third-sexed, and branded permissible targets for ritualistic, collective, and sexualized punishment. A fate that even queer men tend to be spared.

Secondly and perhaps more importantly: the 'misandry' of the average transmisogynistic feminist is *greatly* overstated.

Trivially, we can note how the modern Gender-Conservative movement is full of men and the women who gleefully encourage their violence against trans people, a modern incarnation that bears the most threadbare of claims to *any* feminist tradition. They are, more than anything, a project concerned with the obfuscation of the term 'feminist', so that staunchly patriarchal ideologues can claim the label simply for promulgating transmisogynistic rhetoric. The face of modern transphobia is a far-flung cry from the academic lesbian feminists of yore, and is these days definitively male. Men abound at transphobic rallies, threaten to follow trans women into bathrooms to beat them, and call for the abolition of transition care in publications the world over.

Is such an answer evasive, though? Surely conservative men's transmisogyny is a mainstream discursive force *now*, but was not the second wave chock-full of misandrist lesbian feminists aiming their ire at trans women? Can we not draw a line from their extremism to modern antifeminist backlash?

To get to the heart of that matter, we have to recall a little history.

April, 1973. The West Coast Lesbian Conference was, at that point, the largest gathering of lesbian feminists to date. Beth Elliot, a trans lesbian folk singer and feminist activist had been on the organizing committee for the event and was also scheduled to perform on opening night. Her fellow LA organizers had, in fact, insisted upon it.

When she took the stage at 9 p.m., she was accosted by two women, one of whom snatched the mic away to scream that Beth was a "transsexual" and a "rapist", and demanded that she be ejected. In the ensuing chaos, a few organizers took the initiative to hold a vote (or, two, by some accounts), allowing the assembled audience to decide on Beth's inclusion. The vote passed—by a slim majority, in some accounts, or by an overwhelming two-thirds majority, in some others—and so a visibly shaken Beth Elliot, with the support of her sisters, gave a short performance before promptly leaving.

Robin Morgan, who was scheduled to give a keynote speech on the theme of 'unity' the following day, spent the night editing her address. Rather than speaking for forty-five minutes, Morgan spent twice that time on a meandering screed "attacking everything in sight", per Pat Buchanan—the conference organizers, women who work with men, and of course, *transsexuals*, blaming the continuing ills of patriarchy on a lack of feminist consciousness. Her caustic rhetoric shifted the entire tone and mood of the conference, forefronting the issue of biodestined womanhood. The Black Women's Caucus, who had prepared a position paper on Black feminist organizing and the relevance of race to their struggle, are often omitted entirely from accounts of the conference, in large part due to Morgan's troonmadness sucking up all the oxygen.

While some of the facts surrounding this incident are disputed, we know that Morgan's invective was circulated amongst lesbian feminists, drawing attention to the topic of transsexual inclusion. Her charges that Beth Elliot was an "infiltrator" and "rapist" accrued sufficient cachet to get Beth blacklisted from feminist publications and music scenes. Despite a measure of personal support, Beth withdrew from the public eye, and Morgan's bilious language found itself echoed in 1979's *Transsexual Empire*, this time levied at Sandy Stone.

In some sense, Robin Morgan, Sister Raymond, and their ilk set the discursive tone on translesbophobia. While 1960's *Psycho* attests that the idea of the deceptive, cross-dressing predator already held some sway in the cultural psychosexual imaginary, Morgan and Raymond—clumsily and soporifically—elevated that hateful trope to the status of "feminist concern". They provided a framework and legitimacy to complement the sexologists' pathologization of the "homosexual transsexual", transmuting the cultural idea of the tranny from a pitiable, somewhat tragic figure, to a rapacious and monstrous one. Although coercion through deceptive seduction had always been core to the mythology of transsexuality, Morgan and Raymond enabled eradicationist sentiment towards trans women as a whole to be imbued with a certain feminist authority, recasting it as almost *righteous*.

We were, in the truest sense of the term, *constructed*, remade as biotechnological horrors seeking to traverse, fresh and bloody, from the scalpel to the women's bathroom.

Given the centrality of that hastily-rewritten keynote speech to modern transmisogynistic propaganda, Morgan's awareness of its discursive relevance is fascinating to witness. As Finn Enke notes in *Collective Memory and the Transfeminist 1970s*, when Morgan published her own account in 1977, her comments from the 1973 speech condemning the organizers for "inviting" Beth Elliot are omitted entirely. Morgan deliberately edited the speech to extend her critique of transsexuals and Beth Elliot specifically, dubbing them "gatecrashers" who sought to undermine and destroy the feminist movement from within. She consciously chose to erase Beth's involvement in organizing the event, in addition to eliding that the majority of second-wave lesbian feminists present chose to defend and protect her.

Perhaps the most telling omission in subsequent accounts of this speech is an interesting detail about Morgan herself. Once she was done berating "women who work with men", Morgan launched an impassioned defense of her *husband*. Before she derided Beth Elliot as a "male gatecrasher" with no place in lesbian feminism, Morgan advocated for her male husband's place in lesbian feminism, on the grounds that he was a "feminist", a "feminine man", and—I still cannot help but marvel at this term whenever I encounter it—an "effeminist faggot".

Seriously.

It is impossible to overstate just how utterly pathetic this pantomime of radicalism is. Morgan sublimated her own sexual and gendered anxieties into unrestrained transmisogyny, as many people often do, seeking to secure her own place as a lesbian by defining her legitimacy against the seeming illegitimacy of an "outsider". Her arguments for doing so hinged on staining transsexual womanhood with the original sin of reproducing manhood, even as she pleaded the case that her husband, through his proximity to the feminine, had successfully absolved his own! Morgan's audacity and insecurity drips off the page, revealing her charade to be nothing more than a performative, incoherent, inconsistent, bigoted farce.

Additionally, this revelation demonstrates how even here, in the holy of holies, at the epicenter of lesbian-feminist transmisogyny, *misandry* could hardly be claimed as a motivation. Beth Elliot was condemned for her *transsexuality*. Her putative 'manhood' was invoked only to degender and dehumanize her, while the avowed transmisogynist slurring her asked for the inclusion of men in the same breath!

Nor should we discount those who stood by Beth Elliot and Sandy Stone, even if their efforts were ignored, silenced, and erased. Enke's paper meditates on a photograph of Beth on stage, framed to depict her alone, isolated, besieged. The woman holding Beth's hand is left just out of the picture.

Meanwhile, for all their condemnation of trans lesbians' "male energy", the transmisogynists who so revile trans women's "manhood" had no compunctions when it came to allying with the "male institutions" that have surveilled us, vilified us, marginalized us, and tried to erase our very stories, our connections, our *sisterhood* from history. Even the scraps that remain cannot escape reframing, rewriting, revisionism that insists: *you were always unwanted, and stood apart.*

Except when we weren't, and didn't.

## Radicalized Feminist

Of course, even if "radfem misandry" were the beating heart of feminist transmisogyny, it bears repeating that the radical feminist tradition is not a particularly well-known or influential one today. Ideas such as "gender is a social construct" and "heteronormativity" are uncontroversial in modern feminism, but their radical feminist roots are rather obfuscated, in addition to the foundational tenets of sex-class theory and heterosexuality as a political regime being far from widespread.

Indeed, for all the gesturing at gender-as-social, the average person conversant in pop-feminist jargon retains solidly essentialist notions. "Gender is social, but *sex* is innate," goes the common-sense adage, allowing even "trans allies" to leave their conception of natural, immutable sex untouched. Many cis people are all too comfortable declaring that trans women are "male women" or that "no one believes trans people change sex", statements that go hand-in-hand with the widespread ignorance, misinformation, and indeed propagandized scaremongering surrounding the topic of trans healthcare. Whilst it would no doubt be an excellent party trick, I did not sprout tits through my sheer mastery of the social fabric. I had to take oestrogen for that.

Bluntly, the popular conception of trans people today is frustratingly concomitant with historical tropes regarding us as pitiable wretches who engage in elaborate costuming to make up for the tragedy that is our unchangeable birth sex. Many seem mystified at the thought that we alter our embodiments on a more fundamental level than clothing and address, and learning the degree to which hormones alone can enable trans people to 'pass' tends to elicit discomfort.

Epistemic injustice and the silencing of trans perspectives certainly plays a role, but more concerning is the extent to which transphobic ideologues are allowed to dictate the discourse on trans issues without encountering a meaningful counter-narrative. I've often observed that if a Gender-Conservative insists that trans people do not change sex, the well-meaning ally agrees implicitly, though is quick to remind that trans people do change our *gender*! Both the eradicationist and the ally are in agreement that transness is this superficial, social charade, and seem to principally deviate on the extent to which trans people's delusional performances ought to be humored.

Such an attitude is most evident the second a 'trans ally' happens upon a most disconcerting, destabilizing concept: a trans person who *disagrees* with them! Or worse, one who has her own thoughts, opinions, and perspectives on trans issues that challenge normative assumptions about her life and self-conception. The first time you witness a cis person call a trans woman "TERF" for insisting that she changed her sex, or for describing herself as a "transsexual", the spectacle elicits a hearty chuckle. The absurdity and novelty quickly wears off around the dozenth-or-so time.

That the label of "TERF" can be levied against a trans woman who insists upon her own sex is a function of the total cultural victory of the Gender-Conservative project. Feminism has been indelibly associated with transphobia, transmisogyny is considered a function of 'misandry', and the trans woman is instrumentalized as a voiceless pawn by a myriad of cultural forces that seek to exploit her symbolic significance. The conservative antifeminist can point to her as a consequence of leftist overreach threatening the most fundamental underpinnings of society's (patriarchal) organization, while the liberal antifeminist can use her woes to bemoan how unfair and extreme feminism has grown towards *men*, advocating for an ever-kinder, ever-gentler feminism even as abortion rights are undone and ideological investment in rape culture resurges.

After all, that is one thing the conservative and liberal and even leftist man have always agreed upon: the woman's rightful place, and the necessity of silencing her attempts to protest it.

This environment is not merely conducive for transmisogynistic radicalization, but is one where it absolutely thrives. Imagine, if you can, what it is like to be a woman keenly aware of her culture's intensifying misogyny. Young men—not simply the men "from a different time"—are growing disgruntled with the financial independence that allows women to be more selective in matters of dating and marriage (if they choose to marry at all!). "Men's Rights Activism" is increasingly becoming a part of mainstream conservative politics, and media figures engaging in patriarchal extremism are becoming normalized. In addition to targeting abortion access, reactionaries are openly organizing against contraception, no-fault divorce, and even women's right to vote! Openly male-supremacist politics have not been this popular in decades.

All the while, the media is obsessed with the plight of men, running article after article on the 'male loneliness epidemic' and lamenting the 'feminization of education' that has them giving up on college. It appears having to compete with women who value autonomy over 'traditional family' has soured men on the very idea of upward mobility. Even anti-capitalist politics are taking on a chillingly antifeminist bent, with women's issues dismissed as "idpol", a mere distraction from the primary contradiction of class.

Amidst all this, the topic of trans people seems to come up over and over, given outsize emphasis relative to how many of them there seem to be. Publications of repute run stories constantly, sounding the alarm on the threat "men in dresses" pose to women's bathrooms, sports, prisons, shelters—to the very notion of a sex-segregated space. This deluge is accompanied by a discursive environment where any mention of feminism seems to invite accusations of being a "TERF", a nebulous charge levied at anyone who even mildly suggests that men are systemically empowered to exploit women.

The lip-service paid to trans issues on the left, by those who outright dismiss feminist concerns, in tandem with the barrage of misinformation and the near-total exclusion of trans voices and self-advocacy, leaves the field wide open for Gender-Conservative recruitment.

An oft-overlooked factor in the appeal of hate movements is that they *feel good*. The politics of male grievance has wide appeal to men who, faced with an increasingly hostile world that is unashamedly denying them the economic security their fathers enjoyed, turn to misogyny as an outlet. Sublimating impotence, despair, and rage into organized hate, directed at a target you can actually hurt, who is actually within reach—unlike the faraway, untouchable concept of 'the ruling class'—provides an immediate psychic relief that "class-consciousness" simply cannot rival.

There is a similar kind of unrestrained, psychosexual *glee* among the radicalized women who eagerly turn to the Gender-Conservative pipeline and make the tranny an effigy for all the male figures who have actually done them harm. Organized groups surveil trans people online and collate their social media interactions, distributing the material for adherents to leer at and mock, a *Der Sturmer* for the information age. Post-surgery images are mined for their apparent shock value, and long-forgotten misogynistic invective such as "axe wound" is resuscitated to be applied, anew, to the spectacle of the 'mutilated' trans woman.

Indeed, the chief utility of the trans woman here is as a lesser, *failed* woman at whom one can justifiably direct misogynistic abuse, while simultaneously chastising her for 'perpetuating patriarchal stereotypes'. If she is too feminine, she is a sex-role upholding handmaiden, or she is a "man in drag" if not feminine enough. The trans woman, no matter her deeds, words, or politics, can be tied to the stake and set aflame, over and over. She is a pressure-valve for women looking to hurt something the same way they've been hurt—and feel 'feminist' for doing so. Trans women are *just* male enough for misogynistic abuse directed at them to 'not really count', or to even feel like 'punching up'.

After all, who's going to stick up for us? The same 'allies' who rush to call us 'male-socialized' the second we assert ourselves or act like we deserve dignity?

That is the reality of trans advocacy today. In an era of utter institutional capture, even those who believe themselves to be on our side tacitly endorse the transmisogynistic consensus.

How could this have happened? I mean, the picture of the horse was captioned 'chair'!

Should have been a slam dunk, right?

## Just Answer the Damned Question

Last year, I chose to participate in a mediated conversation with a self-described 'moderate' GC, who claimed to be interested in the transfeminine perspective. 'Moderate', here, refers to the contingent of Gender-Conservatives who had somehow conned themselves into believing their virulent hatred of trans women was in fact a feminist crusade, and were growing increasingly alarmed at the overtures towards and alliances with right-wingers that movement leaders were making.

It was a short exchange. While she was kind enough to not use any slurs, the GC could not help but ask insistently, "How are you different from a gay man, though?"

Wasn't what I experienced really homophobia, not misogyny?

Amused, I brought up my complete lack of attraction to men, and pointed out that I wasn't seen as a man in public. I hadn't been seen as such for some time, in fact. Regrettably, I could not deny biological reality for the sake of her feelings.

I never got a reply to that.

A colleague of mine has opined that GCs exhibit a sort of "nationalistic protectionism" regarding sex-categories. Even when the GC was willing to acknowledge my oppression under patriarchy, I still had to know my place and make it clear I understood that I wasn't *really* a woman. I could be the closest thing to a woman-shaped male individual that her schema allowed, but I must not insist on tainting the purity of Womanhood by claiming it included me.

If I could just concede that sex was essential, impermeable, immutable, then she'd meet me halfway.

That is what The Question is actually getting at. The reason there's no point in debating category errors with a conservative is because *they know they are operating under a limited, exclusive definition.* Conservatism is an *exclusionary ideology,* by *choice,* by *intent,* by *design.* You cannot shatter someone's worldview with an epic burn about imperfect classification, when their classification was never meant to be perfect.

A Gender-Conservative *knows* what a woman is the same way *you* know what a woman is, because *we all fucking know what a woman is.* Their definition of 'woman' is the patriarchal definition of woman: a member of the subordinate sex-class whose domestic, reproductive, and sexual labor is meant to be exploited by the hegemonic sex-class.

Truthfully, Gender-Conservatives have always demonstrated a thorough knowledge of gender-as-social. They demonstrate it when they degender women of color or queer women for not falling within their narrow schema of femininity. They demonstrate it every time they feminize and "unman" any man whom they deem insufficiently reactionary. They are perfectly aware that gender is a social enforcement mechanism because they themselves wield it as one.

Is sex mutable or immutable to a GC, then? If you've finally realized that seeming contradictions do not matter to them, you'll also see that for a GC, it's *neither*.

For a Gender-Conservative, sex under patriarchy is *policed*.

When you're being asked what a woman is, you're not actually being asked for a perfect definition that includes all cis and trans women. (Trust me, I've been ignored after I gave them one.) Look past the words to see the *intent* behind the question, and realize whose *humanity* it is meant to put up for debate. *"What is a woman?"* actually translates to:

"Are you really buying this shit?"

"Listen. You know it's a freak, I know it's a freak. I get that you want to appear all virtuous and high-and-mighty. But c'mon! At the end of the day you *know* what a woman is. I *know* you know what a woman is. And that's not a woman."

"How long are you going to keep humoring it?"

Just until I decide to voice an opinion, usually.

The question is meant to remind you that trans women are *male women*, that we *don't change sex*, that *we don't really experience misogyny*. It is meant to evoke a shared understanding that our genders are *inauthentic*. When a GC asks this question, they're asking whether the person they're questioning really thinks that trans women are worthy of respect as women, are worth taking seriously, or are worth *defending*.

Frankly, when push comes to shove, most people reveal that they don't.

Men's investment in transmisogyny is easily understood, but transmisogynistic women, especially GC women, display an interesting aspect to theirs. To a degree, the idea that a male person could ever experience misogyny, *actual misogyny* like they do, is existentially terrifying. A world where patriarchy is natural, biological, and absolute is an unfair world, an unhappy world, but it is still a world with *order*. A world where even *male anatomy* doesn't guarantee a freedom from misogynistic violence, where gender is proven to be unstable and revocable, confronts them with the reality that their place in the gender hierarchy is only so stable, too.

The tranny is a reminder of how women with no reproductive utility are treated, and the idea that they could share a classification with us—that it is possible for them to be considered *the same kind of thing* as us—is unconscionable.

"A woman is not the same thing as a *mutilated man*," you can almost hear them hiss, forgetting that their quarrel is with Aristotle and not me.

I wish these folks were receptive enough to understand that their hang-ups are not my cross to bear. For I have never seen myself as a "man, made lesser". A failed man? Yes, and proudly so, but *never lesser*. I am, if anything, man perfected in form and spirit, in a way only a being who fulfills her true potential can be.

Faulty conceptions of trans womanhood are a recurrent point of failure for feminisms past and present. When presented with the dilemma that is the trans woman, most people have chosen to recoil in horror and emphasize their separation from us, rather than accept the notion that we might have common cause. Our revelation of gender's porosity is sometimes regarded with a macabre fascination, often fetishized, but rarely taken as proof that our point of view is one worth considering.

We are, currently, at just such an inflection point. The trans moral panic has been (predictably) revealed to be a singular facet of a wider patriarchal agenda to retrench male-supremacy and regulate people's gendered autonomy under the heterosexual regime. Under these nativist, natalist logics, the state cannot permit reproductive assets any bodily autonomy, and must deny them the right to shape their own sex. Your body is a resource for The Nation to mine, and will be legally enshrined as such.

Which leaves you with a choice.

You can take the same option that many have taken before you, time and time again. You can tell yourself that if you agitate loudly enough against her and declare that you are nothing like her, distinguishing yourself sufficiently from the trans woman will spare you her fate. You can try to convince yourself that if you sacrifice some bodies to the gaping maw of the beast, surely it won't hunger for yours.

Or, on the other hand.

You can declare, for the first time in history, that maybe the tranny has a right to exist. That maybe, her freedom to determine her embodiment is indelibly tied to yours. That maybe, just maybe, she's worth fighting for.

And we can see just how far advocating for a radical gendered autonomy takes us.

## About the Author

Talia Bhatt is a radical transfeminist writer of both fiction and nonfiction books. Her debut novel *Dulhaniyaa* is a Bollywood-inspired lesbian romcom that also takes a harsh look at the totality of India's lesbophobia, a romance that grapples with the pain of epistemic erasure. She can be found on Bluesky and Substack, working on this book's sequel and expressing a few too many opinions, and currently resides in the UK with her loving wife.

**You can connect with me on:**
- https://taliabhattwrites.substack.com
- https://bsky.app/profile/enkiducoin.bsky.social

Printed in Great Britain
by Amazon